WENDELL

WENDELL

CROSSING OVER

WENDELL SAILOR

Published by ABC Books for the
AUSTRALIAN BROADCASTING CORPORATION
GPO Box 9994 Sydney NSW 2001

First published March 2003

National Library of Australia
Cataloguing-in-Publication entry
Sailor, Wendell

    Wendell : crossing over

    Includes index
    ISBN 0 7333 1231 4

    1. Sailor, Wendell. 2. Wallabies (Rugby team). 3. Brisbane Broncos (Football team).
    4. Rugby League football players - Australia - Biography. 5. Rugby football
    players - Australia - Biography. 6. Rugby football - Australia - Biography. 7
    Rugby League football - Australia - Biography. I. Australian Broadcasting
    Corporation. II. Title

796.333092

DESIGN / TYPESETTING Reno Design / Graham Rendoth R22063
JACKET PHOTOGRAPHS Front: Nick Wilson / Getty Images; Back: Dave Hunt / AAP Images
SET IN 11/18pt Nofret Light with Bank Gothic and Eurostyle Extended
COLOUR REPRODUCTIONS Colorwize, Adelaide
PRINTING Printed and bound in Australia by Griffin Press, Adelaide

5   4   3   2   1

For my father, Daniel

CONTENTS

11 A glorious gamble

14 New sport, new culture

20 Benny and the Broncos

26 My dilemma: To go or not to go?

33 League World Cup: Decision time

42 The die is cast

53 Sarina boy

60 Ups and downs

67 Not a question of colour

73 In at the deep end

82 One of the Reds

87 Super 12 debut

95 Sin-binned

101 The long wait for a try

108 Campo and me

114   Road rage and the Waratahs

120   A Wallaby at last

128   The pinnacle

136   Post-mortem

146   Tara

152   Two codes: A player's comparison

157   A few of my favourite union people

166   League versus union?

175   My wish list of recruits from league

181   Shaken up by Eddie Jones

187   Trials of a convert

198   Was it all worthwhile?

205   Switching codes: what lies ahead?

212   The best is yet to come

218   Index

WEN

DELL

A GLORIOUS GAMBLE

Switching to rugby union has been the biggest gamble of my life by far. It all started with a small idea that began to bounce around in my head one day a few years ago and kept on bouncing. Where did the idea come from? I know the answer to that exactly. It was June 2000, and I was sitting at home in Brisbane reading the sport in one of the papers. I've always been a big reader of articles about sport. Not just league, but cricket, union, golf, AFL, soccer, even netball. If I enjoy an article or find it particularly interesting for some reason, I'll often read it two or three times over. Anyhow, this day I happened to be reading a rugby union article written by John Eales, who had come up with a 'wish list' of league players he'd like to see switch to union. There were 10 names in the list, and I was one of them. This is what Eales said about me: 'Has had some rugby experience in England and would be a gem. Of great value is his ability to hit the line at pace and often. Is always looking for work and is a Ben Tune type.'

'Would be a gem'! That got me interested. I suppose I felt flattered that the captain of the Wallabies would think I could make a good union player. I finished the article and was about to turn the page when I stopped to think again about what Eales had written. Could he be right? Could I do in union what I'd done in league? Could I make the Wallabies and become a dual international? For a while I sat there thinking about whether or not this might be possible. Then, somehow, the idea of actually doing it began to form in my head.

Just over two years later, on 22 June 2002, I lined up with the rest of the Australian rugby union team at Colonial Stadium in Melbourne while everyone sang *Advance Australia Fair*. I was about to play my first Test as a Wallaby, in the first of a two-match series against France. My gamble had paid off. It was the proudest moment of my life. In fact, I had trouble controlling my emotions — I hoped this wouldn't show when the television camera moved down the line of players. My one regret was that my father had died less than a year before. While the national anthem was being sung I thought of him and wished he was there to see me. In a way, I had a feeling that he was with me.

It was a big occasion for me, and I guess it was also important for rugby union in Australia, because such a thing had never happened before. Over the years quite a few Australians have become dual internationals by crossing from union to league, but I was the first player raised entirely on league to do it in the other direction. This is something I will always be proud of, especially since I came to union cold, with hardly any previous experience of playing it.

When I did eventually announce that I was going over to union, some league people suggested that I was on an ego trip. They said I was setting out to become an international superstar. If only it had been as simple as that. Ego had nothing to do with it. I just wanted to take on a personal challenge, a challenge I couldn't resist. The challenge was to leave the safety zone of league and chance my arm in a new field, test my ability against a whole new type of opposition. The challenge was also to become a dual international. In other words, it was something I wanted to do for me, not for publicity or for accolades.

When I went across to union, I did not turn my back on league. I love rugby league. I think it's a great game, and I always will. After I changed codes, a Sydney journalist wrote that I might go down in history as a Dally Messenger in reverse. The story is that Messenger took a lot of union players with him when he switched from union to league, and the journalist was suggesting that, close to 100 years later, I might take a lot with me in the other direction. I don't agree. League is just too good a game for this to happen, and I don't believe it will happen. But I would like to think that the opportunity of switching codes, in either direction, will now always be there for those players who are game enough to try.

NEW SPORT,
NEW CULTURE

When I decided to transfer to union I didn't know of one other league player who intended doing the same thing. As far as I knew, I'd be taking the big plunge on my own. I certainly didn't know Mat Rogers would join me later. In fact, when he heard I was thinking about making the move, Mat said to me, 'Wendell, you're not serious: you can't really be thinking of going to union.' When I did eventually cross to union I was followed in quick time by three other league players — Rogers, Nathan Blacklock and Lote Tuqiri. The fact that four big-name players had left league to go to union became a sore point between the two codes. League people took it badly, maybe because this type of thing had never happened to them before. The fact that union people were crowing about it didn't help. They did so much sniping at each other that Ken Arthurson, the former league chairman, called for peace.

I stayed out of the argument. One reason was that I had a foot in both camps, but the main reason was that like most players, I just wasn't interested in buying into this type of argument. League and union fans may argue about which code is better, but you don't often hear this kind of talk from the players. I have found that among the players of the two codes there is a lot of mutual respect. League players follow union and admire union players, and union players follow league and admire league players. This is why after I switched codes my league mates kept asking me about the big names in union. 'What's Toutai Kefu like?' they'd say. Or, 'What sort of bloke is Ben Tune?'

Andrew Johns once asked me: 'How do you think I'd go at union?' I told him I thought he'd go well, and I have no doubt that this is true. As far as I know, Johns wasn't considering a switch to union when he asked that question. Like the other league guys, he was just interested to know about the other code.

I wasn't the first league Test player to switch to union. Andrew Walker had played one league Test (against Papua New Guinea) before he returned to union. Willie Carne, another league Test player, did it before me too, although Willie did not go on to play for the Wallabies. All in all, the move wasn't a big success for Willie. Early in the Super 12 season in 2002 I sat next to him at a Broncos match. He said to me, 'You'll get bored with union after six games. I did. You won't enjoy it.' Now Willie Carne is a great athlete. In fact, next to Anthony Mundine, I'd rate him the best natural athlete I've seen on a league field. So why didn't he make it in union? Only Willie knows that for sure, but my guess is that he didn't have the patience to persevere with it. I also know that he had one or two personal problems at the time, which wouldn't have made things easier. Willie was a confidence player. When he was going well, he looked capable of anything. But I think he found it harder than he expected to adjust to union, and he may have lost confidence as a result. If he had stuck at it, I'm sure he would have made as big an impact in union as he did in league.

After it was announced that I was changing codes, Wally Lewis was quoted in the media saying the same thing that Willie Carne had said — that I'd soon get bored with union. I suppose he meant I'd be stranded out on the wing with nothing to do. My attitude is that to some extent it's up to a winger to involve himself in the game, not just wait for the ball to come to him. When I joined the Reds, they made a special effort to find ways of getting me into the game. Daniel Herbert consulted me about it. He asked me to suggest moves that would get the ball to me.

Obviously, there's a cultural difference between league and union, but I find that the difference is bigger between the fans of the two codes, the people who go to the games, than between the players themselves. It's not easy to say exactly what the difference is: it's just something about the way they look, the way they dress, how they react to what's happening on the field, what they yell out to the players. I noticed it early in the Super 12 season in 2002. We played the Auckland Blues at Ballymore on the Saturday night, and next day I went to watch the Broncos. I couldn't get over how different the crowds at the two matches were. The union fans looked well turned out. I don't think any of them wore Reds jerseys. At the league match there were jerseys everywhere — Bronco jerseys and Cronulla jerseys. League has been called the people's game, and I agree with that. I think it was Mat Rogers who called union a corporate game. I know what he meant.

The fact that there is a cultural difference between the codes is probably why each code has some strange ideas about the other. A lot of league followers honestly believe that union is played and watched only by the silver-spoon set — people who went to private schools, drive BMWs and become doctors and lawyers. I used to have that sort of idea about union myself. Whereas nearly all league players are full-on professional footballers, I believed that most union players were university graduates who were just killing time for a few years playing rugby before starting a career as a barrister or whatever.

Some fit this description. One of the Reds' backrowers, Mark Connors, is a lawyer. Another backrower, John Roe, is not far off graduating as a doctor (how he manages to study and play top-level rugby at the same time I haven't a clue). But there are also a lot of union players who are professional footballers, just like the league boys. When I signed to go to union, I was determined to be myself — I was not going to try to turn myself into what I thought a union player ought to be. When I actually crossed over, though, I discovered this wasn't an issue. Union teams are made up of all types. Anyone can fit in.

Union and league players themselves, Broncos and Reds, are much the same. In a lot of ways, Toutai Kefu reminds me of Gorden Tallis. They're the same type of player. At training they just do enough: they just cruise around the park, because they know what they can do on the day. In a game, they dominate. They're both powerhouses, both match-winners. Opposing players don't dare take them on.

In the same way, Chris Latham reminds me of Darren Lockyer. Their skills are different, but they both play the same energetic type of game. They both have a touch of brilliance. They're both capable of pulling off the unexpected and maybe turning the match around.

I found that there is mutual respect between coaches in the two codes as well as between the players. The Wallaby coach, Eddie Jones, and my former coach at the Broncos, Wayne Bennett, have a lot of mutual respect. This has been good for me.

Let me explain. After I'd played the two Tests against the French in 2002, I spoke to Wayne Bennett on the phone. He asked me what Eddie Jones thought of my progress, and I told him that I was pretty sure Ben Tune, who'd been injured, would go back on the right wing for the Tri-Nations Cup, which, of course, is what happened. This meant that for the time being I was out of the Wallaby team. I wanted to know what Wayne Bennett thought of my play. He said, 'Bring over the tapes of the games against France and we'll have a look at them together here.'

So I went to Benny's home and watched the tapes in his room. He pointed out that the lines I was running were slightly off, that my timing wasn't quite right, and he did a study of two tackles I missed in the second Test. 'That's terrible,' he said about one of the missed tackles. 'Look, your head position is all wrong.' In the other, I'd been trying to push the French player over the sideline instead of tackle him. Benny said, 'Del, your defence is not a problem, but you should have made those two tackles. The problem was just poor technique, and you can fix that up.'

He looked at another play where I'd made a half-break but then slowed down and looked around. Benny said, 'Mate, you should have scored from that position. You didn't back yourself enough.' This was true. He said, 'When you're getting the ball, I can tell you're worrying about turning the ball over. Del, the best defenders in league couldn't stop you, but when I watch you in union I see you sometimes a bit tentative. You're breaking or half-breaking the line and looking for support.' I agreed. The problem, I explained to Benny, was that I knew the entire rugby public was watching everything I did and I didn't want to make any stupid errors. Benny said, 'Del, don't worry about that. Remember, the best in league couldn't hold you. You've got to keep running: you play your best football when you're trying to score tries, not when you're trying to set tries up.' In other words, he said, I should stop looking everywhere for support and back myself more.

I valued Benny's advice not just because he's such a great football analyst, but because he knows me as a player inside out. Finally, he said, 'Mate, this is what I reckon you should do. When you go back to training with the Wallabies, get one of the blokes you respect and do some one-on-one tackling. Just get your head position going. You're actually grabbing instead of head leading.' Benny was right about this. In league, all you have to do in defence is stop the ball carrier. In union, you also have to try to turn the ball carrier when you tackle him. Knowing this, I'd got into the habit of grabbing instead of really tackling. Or otherwise I'd just try to drive the runner over the sideline instead of tackling him.

Benny spoke to me about various other aspects of my play, and when I left his house I felt many of my problems had been solved.

I told Eddie Jones about my meeting with Wayne. He was fine with that, because he has a lot of respect for Wayne Bennett, too.

BENNY AND
THE BRONCOS

There are two parts to the story of my move to union. One is where I went to — the Reds and the Wallabies. The other is where I came from — the Broncos. To me, one part of the story is just as important as the other. In fact, if I'd been playing for any team other than the Broncos or for any coach other than Wayne Bennett, I'd have found going to union a lot easier. My emotional attachment to them held me back.

For me, Wayne Bennett is outside comparison. There isn't a coach in league like him and, for me, there never will be. Our relationship was so close over so many years that it couldn't ever be repeated. I'm not embarrassed to call him my mentor. He was one of the main reasons I hesitated about switching to union. He knew my personality so well, and he knew so exactly what to say and do to get the best performance out of me that I found it hard to imagine being coached by anyone but him. As a coach, he struck all the right chords with me, just as Alfie Langer struck all the right chords as a team-mate.

Wayne was never rigid in his ideas. He was always ready to change the routine to suit different situations. How come he was so flexible? The answer is that he really listened to other people. He listened to current players, his own players. You'd hear him say: 'Okay, we've got the Roosters this week. How about we have two days off because it was a big match against the Melbourne Storm last week and a few of the guys are physically sore?' In other words, he'd consult us. He listened to former players with bright ideas that they wanted to pass on to him. In fact, he was prepared to listen to anyone with knowledge of the game.

He was also very observant. Some league coaches I know would switch channels if a rugby union match appeared on their television screen. Not Wayne Bennett. He'd sit and watch the play to see if there was anything there he could learn from. He watched a lot of sport, and his mind was open to everything he saw. In my opinion, this was one of the main reasons Wayne Bennett was a great coach. He wasn't locked into one line of thinking. He grabbed hold of any good idea, no matter where it came from, and he was ready to take advice from his players. He didn't wait for us to give it to him: sometimes he'd come to us and ask for it.

The Broncos had what I call a healthy arrogance. We knew how good we were as a team. We had a tradition of winning which we all believed in. Wayne Bennett used to say to us, 'If you play well, no team can beat you.' We really believed that to be true. It didn't mean we were invincible, because if we didn't play well there was every chance we'd get beaten. We respected the other top teams, we never underrated them, but we honestly believed we could beat any of them if we played as well as we were capable of playing. When I sat in the Broncos' dressing room before a match and looked around at the other blokes sitting there — Gorden Tallis, Alfie Langer, Lote Tuqiri, Darren Lockyer, Shane Webcke or whoever — it wasn't hard to believe in our ability to win.

I believed the Broncos raised the bar for the entire competition, which is why everyone wanted to beat us. We used to hear this from players who joined the Broncos from other clubs. No matter if it was the Cowboys or Newcastle or Parramatta, the team they wanted to beat most of all was the Broncos. We set the standard. If any of the others could beat us, they knew they really were good.

The Reds have a powerful tradition, too, but it's a different type of tradition. You don't find the same arrogance there that you do with the Broncos. What you find is more of a pride in what the Queensland rugby team has done over the years. There's a strong link with the past, a type of bond with former Queensland players. Tony Shaw, who played for Queensland and captained Australia, came in and presented me with my first Reds' jersey. Paul Carozza, the former Wallaby winger, came in, and so did Andrew Slack, another Wallaby captain. All this produces a culture that makes you feel that you have a lot to live up to, that there's a great Queensland record and traditions you have to try hard to maintain.

But the Broncos had something that I don't believe you would find in any other team in any code of football: if you were part of the Broncos, you really felt you were part of a family. In fact, you had to be part of the Broncos to realise how much a family they were. Being part of that family was for a long time one of the most important things in my life, and, strangely enough, even today, long after I left to go to union, I still belong to the family. This is why Alfie Langer phoned me nearly every week during my first Super 12 season to see how I was going and why Gorden Tallis did the same. Even Tony Carroll, a Bronco who went to play league in England, used to call regularly from there to see how I was getting on and wish me luck. In fact, nearly all the Broncos I played with, past and present, have kept in touch with me since I left to play union.

Others who have left the Broncos have been drawn back to the family just like me. When Alfie Langer went to England, he was still in close touch with us — and he eventually came back to the Broncos. Andrew Gee was the same. Peter Ryan went to union and joined the Brumbies, but he's kept in contact. Towards the end of my last season with the Broncos, Peter Ryan came back to train with the Broncos while he was playing club rugby in Brisbane. Even though you might leave the Broncos, you don't really leave the family.

I said before that the Broncos had a tradition of winning. They had another tradition: train hard, play hard and drink hard — and this meant drinking together. I believe that Wayne Bennett had a lot to do with starting this tradition (even though he's not a drinker himself), and it was promoted by blokes like Alfie Langer. If we played on Friday night we'd make a night of it after-wards. No matter what, we all had to be at swimming training at 8.30 next morning; some blokes would stagger home at 5 o'clock, and some wouldn't finish up at the casino until 6.30.

This was a big part of the Broncos' culture. It got the boys to pull together, because as well as having a good time we'd be talking among ourselves about the match we played and about how we could do better next time. We'd go out together whether we won, lost or drew. This was because we didn't take the result too seriously — we didn't go into mourning if we lost, like some other teams I know. I think we picked this up from Wayne Bennett. He didn't like losing, but he didn't brood over a loss.

The Broncos' culture showed up in the way we played. The

Brumbies are much the same: they have a special culture, too. I can tell this from how they play the game, and I've been watching them play for some years now. When the Super 12 began, all of us in the Broncos started watching it. The Brumbies quickly developed a big following among the league guys, maybe because the Brumbies played more like a league team.

Obviously, their coaches of the last few years, Rod Macqueen and Eddie Jones, have had a lot to do with creating the Brumbies' special culture. Senior players like George Gregan and Owen Finegan must have also had a lot to do with it. In my experience, senior players can have a tremendous influence on the rest of the team, on and off the field. In the case of the Broncos, the senior players in my time were Alfie Langer, Gorden Tallis, Darren Lockyer, Shane Webcke and myself. We'd sit down together regularly and discuss the team and what needed to be done.

After I switched to union, the Broncos' people were very curious to see how things turned out. They didn't just wonder how I'd cope with union. They wondered how union would cope with me. I had a reputation in league for being a bit flamboyant, and maybe the Broncos thought that someone like me, with my type of personality, wouldn't fit into the union mould. One of them said to me, 'Del, make sure you don't change the type of person you are to suit them.' I didn't have to. I always try to get on with people, and I also try to be up-front and honest with them. I did my best to be like that when I joined the Reds. I didn't try to change the way I behaved — what they saw was what they got — and I felt I was accepted just as I was. I can't remember a single Queensland player showing resentment at the fact I'd gone straight from league into the Reds on what the media was calling a big contract. Certainly, nothing was ever said to my face.

Whatever the future holds for me as a footballer, I know for sure that when my playing days are over I'm going to feel proud that I played for the Reds and for the Wallabies. I'm also going to feel proud that I was one of Wayne Bennett's Broncos.

MY DILEMMA:
TO GO OR NOT TO GO?

It was June 2000 when John Eales's article put the idea in my head that I might go over and play rugby union. It seemed a far-out idea at first. Why would someone who was brought up on rugby league, who loved rugby league, who loved the team he was playing for, who thought the world of his coach … why would someone like that want to risk everything by switching to union? Until that moment I hadn't given one second's thought to the possibility of ever leaving the Broncos, much less leaving league. My relationship with the coach, Wayne Bennett, was so close that I had never seen myself playing for any team but his. But the idea of a switch to union was now planted in my head, and the more I thought about it the more interested I became.

From the start I could see a couple of huge obstacles. One was that I was a league man through and through. Some other league players had already moved across to union — people like Willie Carne, Andrew Walker and Duncan McRae — but all these blokes had grown up playing union, so they had an instinct for the game. I didn't. I didn't ever play union as a boy. In fact, I don't think I even watched a game of union until I was about 20 and already playing first-grade league for the Broncos.

My only experience of union as a player, which John Eales referred to in his article, was in England in 1998, when I spent the off-season at Leeds. What happened was that a two-year deal to play league with Wigan fell through. I was sorry about that, because it was a terrific deal. The Wigan people virtually asked me to name my price, and they were prepared to lay everything on for me — luxury car (Mercedes or BMW), accommodation and so on. They weren't being generous. They'd done their sums and worked out that I'd increase the gates by enough to make it worth their while. Going to Wigan meant that I'd have to leave the Broncos and give up my Test jersey, but I was prepared to do that. This was the first time since I joined the Broncos that I'd faced up to the fact that I might not stay with them for the rest of my playing career. Looking back now, I suppose it was a sign that I was getting restless, but I wasn't conscious of this at the time.

I was still keen to play in England in the off-season, and this was why I agreed to go to Leeds. It was a way of getting the whole thing out of my system — or so I thought then. By this time I was already attracted to the idea of playing union in England in the off-season. It was more out of curiosity than anything. I knew that a number of top league players in Britain had gone across to union — people like the Paul brothers — and like a lot of league guys, I'd been watching Super 12 ever since it started as the Super 10 competition. But at this stage I was just flirting with union, just wanting to try it and see what it was like. I definitely hadn't given any thought to the idea that I might actually switch codes.

My manager at the time, Barry Collins, organised the contract at Leeds. I had to play two games of league and about 14 games of union. Officially, I didn't get paid for playing union, just for the two games of league, but it all worked out the same financially. I was surprised by how much I enjoyed playing union, and while I obviously knew I had a long way to go before I mastered it, I did come away thinking it was a game I could be successful at. Because I already had a high profile in the north of England as a league player, extra people came to watch me play. On some days, attendances rose from a few hundred to a few thousand.

In my first few games of union I found it hard to make any inroads, and I remember thinking to myself after those games that union wasn't for me. But then I scored five tries in one game and three in another, and suddenly my confidence was up. All in all, in those 14 or so games of union I scored about 15 tries, and even though it wasn't always union of the highest class, there were plenty of talented players on the field, including some past and present internationals, and a few of them did their best to make life difficult for me on the field. In one of my last games, against Leicester, there were a few big-name internationals on the other side. The England captain, Marty Johnson, was one of them, and former England hooker Richard Cockerill was another. The Springbok five-eighth Joel Stransky — who is a very nice guy, incidentally — played for Leicester that day. As I recall, Stransky slotted 10 from 10, and we were beaten by about 45 to nil, but the experience made me think how good it would be to be a top union player with the freedom to play all over the world — France, Italy, Ireland or wherever.

So the rugby experience at Leeds did give me a taste for the game, although, as I said before, I don't think the idea of actually switching to union ever entered my head at that time. If someone had said to me then that I might one day leave the Broncos to play union, I would have laughed at him. My parents would have laughed at him, too. But by July and August 2000, when the idea of switching to union was well and truly in my head, I began to size up how much I'd really learned about playing rugby union during those months at Leeds. I had to admit that it wasn't much. The bottom line was that I'd be starting from scratch if I moved to union — I'd be a duck out of water.

When I put a total media ban on at the Broncos later in the same year [2001], well, that was one of the best times of all. My quotes weren't in the newspapers. I wasn't seeing myself on the TV. It was truly a beautiful thing. Look, I talk to the press all my life. My regret about not talking to the press in the last few months of the 2001 season was that I couldn't give Wendell Sailor the accolades that I wanted to give him. Big Wendell was leaving the Broncos for rugby union after giving the club magnificent service, excitement and greatly adding to our history.

WAYNE BENNETT, FROM HIS BOOK, *DON'T DIE WITH THE MUSIC IN YOU.*

The other problem that really stood out was having to leave the Broncos. The Broncos were far more than a team to me. They were friends and family combined, and I could not bear the thought of cutting myself off from them. Furthermore, I had finally got to the top there: I was looked upon as one of the top players. I realised I'd made it when Wayne Bennett came to me one day — I think this was in 1998 or 1999 — and told me that I was now an automatic selection. 'You're a proven match-winner,' he said. Coming from him, this was the ultimate praise. Leaving the Broncos would mean leaving all this behind, everything I had worked for years to achieve.

It was suggested later that I switched to union because I'd gone as far as I could go in league and had nothing left to achieve there. This wasn't true. Alfie Langer, Kevin Walters and Wayne Bennett all used to say there were two hard things in league. One was getting to the top. The other, which was just as hard, was staying there. I'd managed to get to the top. Now, the challenge was to stay there — to hold onto my place at the top as long as I could. This was quite a challenge, and I was keen to take it on. Switching to union now, it seemed to me, would be leaving the job half done.

So I did my best to close my mind to the idea of leaving league, although over the next few months — the second half of 2000 — I did keep watching the Wallabies. This made a big impression on me. Whether the Wallabies were playing New Zealand, South Africa, England or France, the result was always in doubt, because each of these countries was capable of beating each of the others on any given day. So an international between the Wallabies and any of the other top rugby nations was always a genuine contest, a real battle, and whenever I watched the Wallabies I found myself getting emotionally involved with the team — getting high on patriotic feelings.

The contrast with league was obvious. Australia was so far ahead of the other two countries that to play the game at a reasonable standard you couldn't honestly say an international competition existed at all. New Zealand did rise to the occasion against us every so often, but we always felt we had the better of them. England hardly had a chance against us. I remember one match in 1999 when we beat England by 40-odd points. Although I scored a 90-metre try, I didn't get too excited about anything that day.

As I turned all this over in my head I became aware that there were other things pushing me in the direction of union. I wanted to prove that all the people who were already predicting I'd be a failure in union were wrong. I heard from people in union that I'd be a fish out of water once I made the switch. I heard from people in league that I'd be 'back in a year'. This was more or less what Gorden Tallis, one of my best mates in league, said to me. Gordy was dead against me going to union, and after his neck injury in 2001 I remember him saying what a pity it was that we might never play together again, since he'd be out injured and I'd have gone to union. Then he said, 'But maybe you'll be back in two years'. At the time Gordy probably thought I would be back, but he was still one of the league players who got right behind me once I'd made the switch.

Another of union's big pluses for me was that I could, with any luck, spend the last few years of my football career playing in France, Japan, Italy — pretty well whatever place took my fancy. This idea really appealed to me, and it was a major consideration when I finally decided to throw in my lot with union. In other words, union offered me a pathway to the future. If all went well, my plan was to make the Australian team, play with the Wallabies for a few years, retire from representative rugby and play for a few more years in Italy, Japan or some other country that appealed to my wife, Tara, and me, then return to Australia and take up a job in the media, play a lot of golf and spend plenty of time with my family. At the time all this was no more than pie in the sky, but at least it was something to wish for.

Union had another big attraction for me, which isn't easy to describe in words. I can only call it the culture of rugby: a kind of spirit that seems to surround the game wherever it is played. I'm sure it's this spirit that produces the tremendous atmosphere you find at all rugby internationals. I used to sense the rugby culture just watching the Wallabies play on television, and I had a strong urge to be part of it. I cannot explain why: I just did.

My mind was still wrestling with all these thoughts when I left with the Australian league team to play in the 2000 World Cup in Britain. Up to this point I'd kept the fact I was thinking of changing codes more or less to myself. I'd talked it over with Tara, but with hardly anyone else. On a tour, though, it's hard to keep this kind of thing a secret. It all came out during the tour, which forced me to make some hard decisions.

LEAGUE WORLD CUP: DECISION TIME

I was named player of the tournament at the end of league's 2000 World Cup, and I was named man of the match in the final, an award that really made me feel I had reached the pinnacle in league. I took a lot of pride in the fact that I had been chosen ahead of players of the calibre of Andrew Johns, Gorden Tallis, Darren Lockyer and Trent Barrett. If I could be rated ahead of players like these, even for one match or one tournament, it seemed to me that I must have made it at last.

At the start of the World Cup in 2000, we played England at Twickenham. About 30,000 spectators came along to watch, which we thought wasn't a bad crowd under the circumstances, because it was a wet day. A week later, in much the same kind of weather, the Wallabies played England on the same ground, and the crowd was 85,000. We'd gone to the north of England by then, and we sat in our hotel and watched the Wallabies' match with amazement. How come we had pulled only a third as many people one week ago, we wondered? Then the Wallabies played Scotland at Murrayfield when it was a couple of degrees below freezing — and they drew 65,000 people. I thought, 'How good is that!' A few of us — Gorden Tallis was one of them, I remember — talked about it at the time. Some were still bagging union as a spectacle, saying that the union boys didn't back themselves enough with the ball in hand, which was why they kicked so much, but I think they were all impressed by the size of the union crowds and also by the excitement and the atmosphere.

I know I was impressed. I thought how good it must be to play for the Wallabies in front of crowds as big and as passionate as that. It also became really obvious to me then that the Wallabies had much more scope for international competition than we did. We only had England and New Zealand to play against, and neither of them until now had given us a lot of opposition. In union, on the other hand, there were maybe five or six national teams capable of beating the Wallabies on any given day.

One other thought came into my calculations. The World Cup was supposed to be the ultimate competition in league, and it seemed to me that if I played really well in it, if I reproduced my best form there, I'd have gone as high in the game as I could go, even if I still had things in league to achieve. I remember suddenly thinking to myself one day, 'If I go well in this tournament, I'm going to switch to union.' So I suppose at that point I'd resolved to change codes, but only if I turned in a top World Cup performance. I tried to push the idea of switching to union to the back of my mind for the time being and concentrate on the job at hand, which was to do my best to help win the league World Cup for Australia.

Our coach, Chris Anderson, and I got on well, and one day during the tour Chris took me aside and asked me what my plans were. He had heard by now that I was interested in switching to union, and he asked me straight out, 'Are you going across or not?'

I said, 'Mate, I don't really want to come over here to England to play rugby league, because I think at 26 I'm too young to do that, but I wouldn't mind trying my hand at union.' He asked why. I told him my reasons: that I liked the challenge of trying to make it in the other code; that I would get personal satisfaction out of becoming a dual international; that I'd like to end my playing days in some rugby-playing country like Italy or France or Japan. I also spoke about the huge crowd the Wallabies had just pulled at Twickenham and said I wouldn't mind being part of an occasion like that. Chris said, 'That's just a rugby cultural thing, but I agree: it would be good to experience something like that.'

On the night before the World Cup final I got only three hours' sleep. The truth is, I suffered an attack of nerves, because I knew how important the match was to me. I had a strong feeling that this match would be the climax of my career in league — that it was what I'd been working towards ever since I started playing league as a kid at Sarina. By now I'd all but decided to transfer to union, and I felt pretty sure this would be the last time I'd play league for Australia, because I couldn't see them picking me again if I'd signed to go to union. Each of us had a room to ourselves where we were staying in Manchester, and I kept getting up to watch television because I couldn't sleep. I even phoned my parents back in Australia around three o'clock in the morning and told them how nervous I was. 'You'll be right,' Mum said. 'Just get out there and play.'

Dawn came eventually, and sure enough, it was cold and wet. As we drove to Old Trafford in the team bus you could hear the rain belting on the roof. One more problem, I thought to myself — a slippery ball. The pressure was on us that day. Australia hadn't lost a World Cup for as long as anyone could remember, so we had a record to maintain, and while we may have been the best team and were confident of winning, there was always a chance in a one-off match that the underdog, New Zealand, would get up.

It was Australian winger Wendell Sailor, who was compared with Eric Grothe by his coach after the game, who made sure of victory. He set up Australia's first try, in the 26th minute, with a clever kick that sat up in the Kiwi in-goal for centre Matt Gidley to score, touched down himself in the 66th minute and scored his second three minutes later. For his second score, he was the beneficiary of some deft brilliance when halfback Brett Kimmorley threw an unsighted pass to Gidley, who tapped the ball out to Sailor. These are skills which Australia's league production line continues to produce and which are the envy of the international game. Sailor might have finished with three, but video referee Gerry Kershaw denied him a try in the first half, ruling he had been held up by second-rower Stephen Kearney by the narrowest of margins. "Stephen Kearney's got a big hand, obviously," Sailor said.

STEVE MASCORD, REPORT IN THE *SYDNEY MORNING HERALD* ON THE 2000 LEAGUE WORLD CUP FINAL.

Despite my nerves, my lack of sleep and the wet weather, I felt pumped up when we finally got out on the field. I had felt that way throughout the whole tournament. We had a lot of very talented people in our team, so it was hard for any one player to stand out, but right from the start of the World Cup my attitude towards the crowd in every match I played was: 'Here I am. This is what I can do.' I was determined to make a big impact on the tournament, and I was particularly determined to make a big impact in the final.

As it turned out, I played the game of my life. Everything I tried to do came off. I don't often kick, but in one of the first plays I dribbled the ball through for Matty Gidley to score. Then I scored two tries in the second half. I thought I'd scored a third, but it was disallowed. If I had scored the try, it would have been the first time that anyone had scored three tries in a World Cup final. When the match ended I felt relieved, more than anything — I'd worried so much about having a bad game that I was just pleased that hadn't happened. At that moment the die was probably cast. My transfer to union was now close to a certainty.

Wendell scored a couple of tries today that only he could have scored. He is one of the best wingers Australia has produced. He is up there with Eric Grothe.

CHRIS ANDERSON, AUSTRALIAN RUGBY LEAGUE COACH, SPEAKING AFTER THE 2000 LEAGUE WORLD CUP FINAL.

After the World Cup final we relaxed for a few days and did a fair amount of drinking. The other league players and our coach, Chris Anderson, all knew I was thinking seriously of switching to union, but I don't think any of them believed I'd actually go. Gorden Tallis had an idea I might be serious, and while he and I and a few other Broncos were having a drink together a day or two after the World Cup final he asked me, 'Mate, how much would you need to stay?' — meaning stay with the Broncos. Now compared with players in some other clubs, the Broncos aren't overly well paid. Because of the camaraderie in the team, and because the guys think so much of Wayne Bennett, and probably because they prefer to live in Queensland, they're happy to keep playing for the Broncos for less than they'd probably get elsewhere. In other words, they need less to stay. It was also a fact that I wasn't on such a big contract with the Broncos. I'd seen other players come to the Broncos on bigger contracts than me, but that didn't bother me. I was happy at the Broncos, and I never felt jealous about what others in the team were earning. If it was more than me, good luck to them!

This time, though, when Gorden Tallis put the question to me, I answered differently. We'd had a fair bit to drink, we'd all been close to each other for a long time, and I suppose we were feeling a bit emotional. I said to Tallis, 'Gordy, you know John Ribot promised me I'd be on a good contract, but I know that other wingers and players have got better contracts than me. As much as I've been happy with the Broncos, it's time for me to get a decent contract. I've done the yards now.' A few other Broncos were listening to this. Darren Lockyer was one. Another was Shane Webcke, who would have known what I was talking about, because he wasn't on such a big contract either. I used to say that

Webby and I were the 'battlers of the Broncos'. We'd both put a lot into the club, but we weren't on the elite contracts most people probably imagined us to be on.

Gorden Tallis asked me again, 'Tell me how much you need.' I told him that to keep me, the Broncos would have to offer me a four-year deal with a lot more money, and I quoted a figure. 'I'm going to ask Benny for it,' I said, 'and if I don't get it I'm out.'

In the crowd were two of the greatest wingers of all time – Welshman Billy Boston and South African Tom Van Vollenhoven, who thrilled English fans in the 1960s. They were introduced at halftime as part of an English 'Hall of Fame' tribute. It is doubtful that the blockbusting Boston, who terrorised Australian teams in the 1950s and 1960s, could have finished any better than Sailor when he was presented with opportunities in the 68th and 70th minutes and scored tries which ended the Kiwi challenge. Sailor said he was shattered when Kershaw ruled against him in the 23rd minute on the basis Kiwi forward Stephen Kearney had got his hand under the ball as Sailor tried to force it.

STEVE RICKETTS, REPORT IN THE *DAILY TELEGRAPH* ON THE 2000 LEAGUE WORLD CUP FINAL.

I remember how things changed from 'I might go to union' to 'I'm thinking seriously of going to union' and finally to 'I'm definitely going.' Wendell jokes a lot, but I never took his talk about going to union as a joke, because I knew he'd got to a point in league – I could see it from the way he was speaking and acting – where something was missing for him. It wasn't that he was bored with league, but he's just a person who thrives on a new challenge. So when he told me he was thinking of going to union, I didn't laugh, because I knew this was something that he'd do.

TARA SAILOR

Obviously, Gorden and the others were doing their best that night to get me to sign on again with the Broncos, which is why they were keen for me to speak directly to Wayne Bennett. This is what we did, probably all sounding a bit tanked: we phoned Wayne Bennett in Brisbane.

When I spelled out the deal I wanted, Wayne said, 'Del, you've arrived as a footballer. Before, you were a great athlete and a good footballer. Now, you're an elite footballer.' I said, 'Benny, I appreciate that. I've had a great time at the Broncos, but, mate, I have to say this: I was promised bigger contracts in the past, and now I want the four-year deal.' He said, 'Del, you deserve it — I think we owe you that.' Hearing this, I told Wayne I couldn't see myself going to union, and when I got off the phone I said to Gorden Tallis, 'Gordy, I'm going to stay.' When I announced this I was hugged and cheered by the rest of the boys, who had been drinking long enough to be high on emotion. I was high on emotion, too.

At the time, what I told Gorden Tallis and the others was true. I still hadn't decided where my future lay, but that night, after my conversation with Wayne Bennett, I was certainly pumped up with the idea of staying in league. In the cold light of morning, though, I wasn't so sure. Soon after I got back to Australia, I gave a press conference where reporters asked me if it was true that I was going to union. I replied that I'd made no decision to switch to union, that I'd been happy at the Broncos and that for the time being I was keeping my options open. All this was true.

THE DIE IS CAST

Thanks to my performances at the World Cup, my career had been given a lift. It didn't take me long after I returned to Australia to realise that I was a bigger name now than I'd ever been before. One result of this was that various management firms began approaching me, wanting me as a client and telling me what they could do for me in the way of endorsements and so on. Until now, my manager had been Barry Collins; he'd been my manager since I was 18. Barry looked after quite a few other league players, among them Kevin Walters and Glenn Lazarus, but he wasn't a rugby union man, and because I was still open to the idea of switching to union (although I was also still basically reconciled to sticking with league), I felt I needed a manager with close connections to that code. I talked to Barry about it, and although he was keen to continue as my manager, he said he would accept any decision I made. So I talked to the various management firms that had approached me — AMI, David Campese Management and one or two others. They all promised to secure a good contract for me and they all seemed to know what they were talking about, so I was faced with a difficult choice.

To complicate matters, I still hadn't made up my mind whether to stay with league or go to union. I had meant what I said when I told Gorden Tallis and the others in England that I'd stick with league, but after coming home I again began to feel the urge to try my hand at union. As the weeks went by, I grew keener and keener on the union option, but I wasn't yet able to make a final commitment.

> *Wendell Sailor had given his all to the Broncos over nine years. He thought it was time, time for him to move – luckily while at the top of his game and by his own initiative. But he had given great service to our club.*
>
> **WAYNE BENNETT**, FROM HIS BOOK, *DON'T DIE WITH THE MUSIC IN YOU.*

I've never been one to make up my mind easily. The bigger the decision, the more I sweat over it, and in the whole of my life I'd never had to make a bigger decision than this one: should I risk everything by going to union? There were so many things on either side to weigh up. I knew my parents would want me to stay in league, and I didn't want to disappoint them. My father had followed league all his life, and I knew how much the Broncos in particular meant to him and Mum. My parents had done so much to help me get to where I was in league that I felt it would be ungrateful of me to leave.

Also, I had no illusions about how tough it would be starting a career in union. I was 26 years old, and apart from a handful of games of union in England, I'd played nothing but rugby league since I was eight years old. I thought there was a chance that if I went to union on a big contract I might be targeted by players who resented the fact that I was maybe earning more money than they were. Worst of all, there was no guarantee I'd be even half as successful in union as I had been in league. There was even a chance I'd be a complete flop, which I would hate more than anything. When I thought of all these potential problems, the idea of staying in league seemed very attractive. In this way I kept going hot and cold on the idea of switching.

When I weighed everything up, though, I nearly always came to the conclusion that, personal feelings aside, going to union was the logical thing for me to do. A sort of natural progression after my nine years as a professional in league. Sure, it was a gamble, but the potential pluses outweighed the minuses. What tipped the balance was meeting with the Brumbies' coach, Eddie Jones, and finding that he was so much like Wayne Bennett. Even at that time, the talk was that Jones was odds-on to become Wallaby coach after Rod Macqueen retired, so there was obviously a big chance I would never play for the Brumbies under him, even if I wanted to.

I can't remember the exact date of that meeting, but it was in late 2000. It was arranged by Anthony Picone of AMI, which by this time I'd chosen as my management firm. He told me Jones would like to meet me to discuss my prospects in union, and I said I'd be happy to meet him. So Jones flew up from Canberra, and I met him one Saturday morning at the Hilton Hotel in Brisbane. We sat and had a cup of coffee, and talked for about an hour. At the end of that hour, I told Anthony that I'd made up my mind: I wanted to play union, I wanted to be coached by Eddie Jones, and so I wanted to play for the Brumbies. I don't mind admitting that I've always been someone who has looked for guidance in life. Wayne Bennett gave it to me when I played with the Broncos. I felt Eddie Jones could steer me in the right direction, too.

Why did Jones impress me so much? I said before that he reminded me a lot of Wayne Bennett. He had the same kind of air about him. The subject of money wasn't even mentioned. Jones just talked to me about what the Brumbies could do for me — and what he thought I could do for the Brumbies. During our meeting I asked him whether I could be sure he would still be coach if I signed on with the Brumbies, because everyone was expecting him to take over as the Wallabies' coach from Rod Macqueen. Jones said he didn't know for sure what his own future would be, but whether he was still the Brumbies' coach or not, the fact was that a system, a culture, was in place at the Brumbies which would guarantee that the Brumbies' playing style would be maintained. I could relate to that: the Broncos had had the same style of play going for 10 years or more.

So the Brumbies were the first rugby people to take an interest in me, and at this point they were the team I seemed likely to play for if I switched. The fact that Eddie Jones was their coach was the main reason. I also liked the way the Brumbies played. To play for the Brumbies, it seemed to me, would be the nearest thing in union to playing for the Broncos. But I was still a full-blooded Queenslander, and until then the idea of living in Canberra had never entered my head. My old Bronco team-mate, Peter Ryan, now a Brumbie himself, phoned me a few times to say that I ought to join him in Canberra if I was moving to union.

The Brumbies would suit me, he said, and I'd probably be fast-tracked if I went there. But living in Canberra did not appeal to me much. I asked Tara how she would feel about living in the cold of Canberra. She wasn't too excited at the prospect either.

I still had a few self-doubts about making the switch to union. One worry was that even if I wasn't a complete flop, I might not get beyond the Super 12 stage. A big attraction for me was the 2003 World Cup. I'd played in league's World Cup in 2000, but I would have to say, without wanting to knock it, that I never felt it was a real world event. I knew rugby's World Cup would be different. It's a genuinely international event, and the fact that this one would be staged in Australia made it hard to resist. I had seen the impact of the Olympics in Sydney in 2000 — I was there when Cathy Freeman won the 400 metres — and I could imagine what the World Cup would be like. I wanted to be part of it.

That meeting with Eddie Jones put a seal on my plans to switch to union. I still felt some reservations about making the move — like everything else, it was sure to have a down side — but I now felt committed to it, 100 per cent. The uncertainty was finally gone. Outside my immediate family, the person I broke the news to first was Wayne Bennett. I told him about my meeting with Eddie Jones. I said, 'Benny, I like him, I like what he has to offer. I'm going to play union for the Brumbies.'

Wayne asked me to keep my options open a little while longer. No matter how much money the rugby union people might offer me, he said, he wanted me to come back to him before accepting it, because the Broncos might be able to match it. I said, 'Benny, I'm not looking at it like that. I don't want to get into some kind of tug of war. I'm grateful for everything league's given me. I've played in great teams — the Broncos, Queensland and Australia.

I've been in teams that have won the World Cup, State of Origins, grand finals. ET (Andrew Ettingshausen) went for 16 years and never played in a team that won a grand final, and I've played in three. So I've a lot to be thankful for, but I just think that at 26 the time has come for me to move on, to try something else and maybe become a dual international.'

Wayne could see things from my point of view and I think he realised at this point that I couldn't be persuaded to stay. He said, 'Del, I don't want to lose you either as a player or a friend, but if going to union is honestly what you want to do then you have my support, because there'll be a lot of life after football, and I hope we'll still be friends then.' That was typical of Wayne Bennett. I've never met anyone in sport I admired more. I didn't agree with everything he did, but we were always honest with each other. There were times when I told him I thought he was wrong. I even questioned his team selections, telling him he was mad to leave so-and-so out or not to give so-and-so a go. He was always honest with me, too. He'd say to me, 'What's wrong with your form at the moment? Are you reading too much about yourself?' I heard him say the same to Gorden Tallis: 'You've been reading your scrapbook, have you, mate?'

But Wayne refused to budge when I asked him if he would release me so I could go to union a year earlier. From memory, this was in early February 2001. I'd started to worry about playing another year of league when it was known that I was going to union. It seemed to me that this could create difficulties for everyone at the Broncos, including myself, and that it would be cleaner and better for all concerned if I left straight away. I also thought that it would be good for me to have two years of top-class union under my belt before the World Cup year, which is what I really had in my sights. I knew that Benny had released other senior players early — Mick Hancock was one of them — so I felt I had a chance. Benny and I had a good heart-to-heart talk about it at his place, but he wouldn't agree. He said he needed me at the Broncos. 'I couldn't do it to the other blokes here,' he said. 'You're a world-class player now. I'd be stupid to let you go.' So that was that.

It was hard for me to leave Wayne, and it was hard for me to leave rugby league. I'd built a reputation and earned respect there over the previous nine years, and now I was giving it all up. I know a lot of people thought that switching codes was easy for me, that I was laughing all the way to the bank. If only they knew! The fact is I could have earned more money playing league in England than playing union in Australia, but I regarded playing in England as something you did for a year or two before you retired, and at 26 I knew I wasn't ready for that yet. For the same reason I think Wayne Bennett was as happy for me to go to union as he would have been if I'd gone to play league in England — that is, not at all. He was dead against the idea of my going to England to play, because he believed I had at least another four years left at my peak and he didn't want me to waste them in England. In other words, he had my best interests at heart.

After my meeting with Eddie Jones, the ARU arranged for me to go to Sydney to see Jeff Miller, who was then their high performance manager. We met at the ARU's office in North Sydney and then went to a nearby coffee shop for a talk. Miller explained to me how the ARU operated and how I might fit into its set-up if I came over. Contrary to a story that was floated later, he definitely did not guarantee that I'd be selected for this or that team and he definitely did not promise me a Wallaby jersey.

In any case, at this stage AMI, my management firm, was negotiating with the ARU over my contract, so while I was talking to Jeff Miller I was careful not to give the impression that union already had me in the bag. I did ask him quite a few questions, and he gave me straight answers. Miller was the first ARU official I'd had face-to-face dealings with, and I came away impressed.

At this stage, towards the end of 2000, I just wanted to sign a deal and know once and for all that I was going to union. But the deal itself had to be sorted out — this seemed to take forever — and there were other financial matters such as endorsements that had to be wrapped up as well. So although I was now personally committed to the idea of playing union, my transfer became an on-again, off-again affair as negotiations between AMI and the ARU dragged on, and it all became a bit frustrating. During this time I often spoke to Wayne Bennett and asked his advice. Wayne was happy to give it.

I had listened to all the options. The different management people who wanted me as a client were all familiar with what my options were worth on the market. They were able to tell me how much I could earn if I stayed at the Broncos, or moved to Sydney and played for someone like the Bulldogs or Roosters, or switched to union, or went to England to play league. By now, though, I was past weighing up options. I told AMI that I didn't want to shop around: I'd made up my mind to go to union and I wanted the deal with the ARU done. Apart from anything else, I wanted to put an end to all the speculation in the media about what I would do. The newspapers kept running stories saying I was virtually certain to go to the Brumbies; that no, I'd probably stay with the Broncos after all; and that it was actually the Waratahs that were about to sign me up. I realised that fans of both codes were getting sick of this. 'If he's going why doesn't he go? If he's staying why doesn't he stay?' they were asking.

At last, in early 2001, the deal was done, and it was announced to the media that I was switching to union. The ARU made the announcement in February 2001, on the day that happened to be the Broncos' fans' day. This probably wasn't intentional, as a lot of Broncos' people suspected it was, but the timing was still a pity, because in the eyes of many Broncos' supporters it made me look even more a traitor than would have been the case other- wise. It is probably only human nature that some people think like this, but it was pretty unfair to me, because I wasn't doing anything to harm the Broncos.

The fact that I would be switching to union was announced in February, but I didn't sign on with the Reds until the middle of that year. What happened during those four months? I made no secret of the fact that I was interested in playing for the Brumbies, preferably under Eddie Jones, but as things turned out, the fact that Jones was leaving the Brumbies to coach the Wallabies wasn't a deciding factor. There was another, more important reason for ruling out the Brumbies. My contract was with the ARU, and it soon became obvious that the ARU preferred me to play with the Reds or the Waratahs. At the time, I guessed this was probably because Sydney and Brisbane were the main league strongholds, and I'd obviously have a better chance of pulling in league supporters if I played for a team based in one of these big cities. I don't know for sure if this was the ARU's plan, but it seemed to make sense to me.

In the end, it came down to the fact that my roots were in Queensland, nearly all my friends and family were there, and I was happy living in Brisbane.

Tara backed my decision to go to union. We had some pretty intense conversations about it while I was in the process of weighing up the pros and cons, and once she satisfied herself that going to union was what I really wanted to do she was behind me all the way. If she hadn't been behind me, I'm not sure I could have gone through with it. Like me, Tara had quite a bit to lose from the change of codes. She had made a lot of friends in rugby league, especially among the wives of other Broncos, and, like it or not, she would probably have to leave some of them behind.

My parents, when they heard that my transfer to union was definite, gave me their blessing, too. Mum said she'd be happy if I was happy. Dad, being a dyed-in-the-wool league fan, found it harder to accept, but he said he wanted whatever was best for me, and if this meant going to union, so be it. I explained to him why I thought going to union would be a great opportunity for me, and I think he could see that, although he did say to me once, 'You're going to miss league but, aren't you?' I replied, 'Yes, Dad, I know I'll miss it, but leaving is still the right thing for me.'

Chris Anderson did not like the idea of my switching to union, but he did not hold it against me in any way, either then or later. This was typical of the reaction I got from most league people when they found out I was going to union: they didn't like it, but they accepted it, knowing it was what I'd set my heart on. Chris Anderson and I remained good friends, and he was invited to my wedding in December 2001, although a heart attack stopped him coming. Before that, while I was still playing league, he'd stood by me.

During 2001, my last year in league, there was a rumour that I wouldn't be picked to play for Australia because I would be leaving to play union at the end of the season. If this had happened, I wouldn't have complained. After all, there were several other top-class wingers to choose from, and the game did have to look to the future. I asked Chris Anderson if I was out, saying that I would understand it if I was. He replied, 'No way. You deserve your spot, Wendell, so as far as I'm concerned you're in.'

SARINA BOY

I'm one of those lucky people who are happy with life, and I think this is because I know where I've come from. My father was a labourer on the railways, not a well-paid job, so paying the bills was always a battle. From the time I first started playing league at the age of eight, Dad nearly always drove me to and from training and to and from matches. When I was in the under-9s and under-10s I used to have to train in Mackay, which was about a 40-kilometre drive from Sarina, and there were times when he didn't have the money to buy petrol for the trip. So he'd borrow the petrol money from a friend, and off we'd go in our old Cortina.

Even as a small boy, as far back as grade one, I was sure I was going to be famous at something. Maybe most boys have dreams of becoming famous one day, but I honestly believed it would happen. I was so certain of it, in fact, that I used to tell my mates at school about it. As far back as I can remember, I always had plenty of self-confidence. If anything, as a boy I had too much confidence. When I was married in December 2001, some of my old mates from primary school in Sarina were guests at the wedding. One of them said to me, 'Wendell, people have got the wrong idea about you. They think you became cocky and arrogant when you became a big shot at the Broncos, but we know you were cocky and arrogant right back in grade one.'

(Kevy Walters tells a story about me when I first arrived at the Broncos as an 18-year-old, at the start of 1993. He says I rocked up, shook his hand and said, 'Pleased to meet you. I'll be playing with you in the first-grade team before the season is over.' I don't remember saying this, but Kevy insists the story is true, so I'll take his word for it.)

At Sarina I played all the sports going — cricket, soccer, rugby league, squash. Here was a typical week for me while I was growing up: on Monday night I'd play junior squash; on Wednesday night it would be senior squash with men or mixed squash with men and women; on Thursday and Friday afternoons I'd go for rugby league training; on Saturday I'd play in a match; and on Sunday I'd do athletics. I didn't realise it then, but I was lucky to grow up in a country town like Sarina and be involved in sport five or six days a week. It kept me out of trouble, and it prepared me for a career as a professional sportsman. If I had grown up in Brisbane, I may never have pulled on a pair of football boots.

The other thing I didn't realise at the time was how much it cost my parents in time and money to keep me playing sport. As well as having to buy my squash racket, my football boots, my football jersey, my mouthguard, my cricket cap and whites, my running shoes and my athletics singlet, Mum spent hours every week cleaning and ironing my various sporting outfits and Dad seemed to spend most of his spare time driving me to and from training sessions and matches in his old car, which I think cost him $5000 second-hand and which he had to keep making payments on.

I did not get my physique from Dad: he was a shortish, thickset person. Unlike me, he was extremely modest and did not have a lot to say. Once, after a few of the Broncos boys met him, they said to me, 'Gee, you're nothing like your father.' Dad used to get up at five o'clock in the morning, start work at six and be home by about 3.30 in the afternoon. He'd barely have time to sit down in the kitchen for a cup of coffee before I'd be pestering him to take me to training at Mackay. I wouldn't let up: 'Come on, Dad — quick, let's go or I'll be late.' Poor Dad would swallow his coffee, drive me for 30 minutes to Mackay, sit there in the car for maybe an hour and a quarter while I was training, drive us home — we'd usually arrive around 6.15 pm — have his dinner, watch a bit of television and be in bed by nine o'clock. In other words, his whole life was dedicated to doing things for his family, not for himself. It was the same with money: I can't ever remember him splurging on himself or on Mum. He saved his money so he could spend on me.

Looking back now, I don't think it ever entered my parents' heads while I was growing up that I might make sport my career. They did what they did for me not because they thought it might pay off financially in the long run, but simply because they thought sport was good for me and they knew I enjoyed it. They did not often refuse me anything where sport was concerned, and when they did say no I sometimes reacted pretty badly, because I had no idea then how tight things were for them financially. I remember asking them once to buy me a Greg Chappell cricket bat, which I think cost about $120. They said no, they couldn't afford it, but I wouldn't accept that. I kept hounding them, asking why they couldn't put it on lay–by and pay it off or how come other kids got new cricket bats and I didn't. In the end I didn't get the bat, and I realise now this was only because they literally did not have $120 to spare.

My parents did not own their home at Sarina. We lived in a railways house — that is, a house owned by Queensland Railways and rented to railway employees. It wasn't a bad house by any means, and all the time I was growing up we were never short of any basics. It was the 'extras' that my parents always struggled to come up with — the Greg Chappell cricket bat, the new pair of Wally Lewis football boots, the trips I had to make from Sarina to play sport. If I was playing cricket for Mackay at Rockhampton, for example, my father would have to drive me to Mackay in time to catch the bus at six o'clock in the morning and I wouldn't get home until that evening, which meant I could need as much as $25 for meals and fares. Sometimes Dad didn't have the $25, but he would always borrow it from somewhere to make sure I had my day's cricket.

My sister, Michelle, left home when she was 18, and for a while after that I was an 'only child'. Michelle had two children when she was young and, for various reasons, my parents took in these two grandchildren, Jasmine and Daniel, and brought them up as their own. So all of a sudden I effectively had a brother and sister just a few years younger than me. I have always admired my parents for taking on the responsibility of raising and supporting those two kids, especially since they were under a fair amount of financial pressure already and were not getting any younger themselves.

As hard-pressed for money as they were, my parents often lent money to other people — either people they knew in Sarina or members of our family. All in all, my father had a hard life, but, as I said to my mother after he died, I did not ever hear him complain about the hand that fate had dealt him.

> 'He was busy talking football. So I said, "Look, Wendell, if you don't do your homework, your grades won't be good enough for you to get a job." He looked me in the eye and said, "I don't need to do homework, sir, because I'm going to play football for the Broncos." He hadn't even played A grade in Mackay. He was a nobody, yet he had absolutely no doubt he was going to be a football star.' Peter McGiffin, Sailor's teacher at Sarina High, recalling a conversation with his 16-year-old pupil.'
>
> QUOTED BY **FRANK ROBSON** IN THE *GOOD WEEKEND*.

I like going back to Sarina from time to time, especially if I find I'm taking myself too seriously, because going back there always brings me down to earth. It's not the same any more without Dad, though. Memories of him are everywhere around Sarina, and one of my favourites is of going fishing with him on the beach. I was the one who used to suggest we went fishing, and I'd have to talk him into it, but once we got to the beach and started fishing I'd always get bored with it pretty quickly and go for a six- or seven-kilometre run on the sand instead. When I came back he'd still be fishing and he'd laugh at me, because it was always the same: I was the one who'd suggest we went fishing and he was the one who fished. Then, while he fished, I'd hang around with him, talking and throwing pebbles into the surf. It was a simple scene, but for me it was pure happiness.

I was almost as good at cricket as I was at rugby league. I made the Mackay team as an opening bowler, and then I was selected for the Central Queensland team, which played against other regional teams. There were a few stars of the future in the teams we played against, such as Jimmy Maher, Andrew Symonds and Martin Love, who were all about my age. Jimmy Maher likes to joke about me as a cricketer, saying how he remembers 'this big, tall, black West Indian paceman' running in to bowl.

When I was playing under-12s and under-13s cricket I fully expected to make the Queensland team, because I was one of the most successful performers in the state carnivals. But I didn't make the Queensland team. In fact, I didn't even make the Queensland Country team, which surprised people who knew me as a player, and definitely surprised me. I used to wonder if they had something against me personally. In the end, it probably didn't matter much, because league was always the sport I was going to concentrate on, but I still rate my failure to make those Queensland under-age cricket teams as one of my biggest disappointments in sport.

Having done so much to help me make it to the top in sport, my parents never asked for anything in return. After I joined the Broncos and began earning good money, I would have been happy if my father or mother had phoned me and said, 'Wendell, we're a bit short at the moment. Could you lend us a few hundred to see us through?' But they never did, even though they must have been short many times. In fact, they never even hinted at it. I did try, off my own bat, to help them where I could, but they were always reluctant to accept help of any kind. One thing I did which I know they appreciated was buy them a new car with my first Super League cheque. Mum cried when she saw it. They'd had to make do with old bombs of cars for so long that, for once, they were happy to accept.

When I first started playing for the Broncos I asked my parents if they'd like to move down to Brisbane and join me. They said no, they were happy where they were in Sarina. As it turned out, this was a good thing for me, because it meant I always had a place to retreat to. Going back there every so often and spending time at the beach, far away from all the hype of being a so-called football star, helped keep my feet on the ground. I used to train every day I was there, even on Christmas Day. In fact, going for a run on the beach on Christmas Day became a kind of tradition. I always associated this Christmas Day run with my father, because he used to drive with me to the beach, and it was the trip to the beach I missed most on Christmas Day 2001, the first Christmas after he died.

UPS AND DOWNS

Actually, I nearly left league once before. That was way back when I was in the under-16s. The year before, in the under-15s, I captained the Mackay team. This year, though, I didn't even make the team. For someone with my pride and ego, it was a terrible blow. I felt I'd had a raw deal, and I thought to myself, 'Stuff it — I'll never play league again.' I told my parents so, and at the time I really meant it. They sat me down and talked to me about it. They told me they could understand my disappointment, but that the smart thing to do, as well as the gutsy thing to do, was to hang in there, to play as well as I could and try to regain my place later in the season.

That is what I ended up doing. I won back my place in the Mackay side, and when we played in the North Queensland final — against Cairns, I think — I was voted man of the match. This whole affair may not sound very important now, but the fact is, I definitely intended to give up league. If it hadn't been for my parents, it's possible I wouldn't have played league again — and who knows where I would have ended up? So deciding to keep playing league was a turning point in my life, and I give my parents the credit for helping me make the right decision.

Later that season I was picked to play in the men's A-grade team for Sarina. The coach had seen me playing in the juniors and asked me if I'd go on the bench for the A-grade men's team next day. I was 16 years old, and the thought of mixing it with some of the big, hard men who played A grade was a bit frightening. I could see myself being snapped clean in half. I sat on the bench until about halfway through the second half, when the coach called to me, 'Mate, you're on.'

On I went — at this stage Sarina was behind by a few points. We were being threatened on our line, and when the ball came to me, I started to run. There was one opposition player directly in front of me, a rough-looking bloke with tattoos on his neck and arms. I stepped around him and started sprinting for the other end of the field. A few opposition forwards chased me, but I had plenty of pace, and none of them got near me. I scored a try under the posts, which turned out to be the winning try.

For a few days after that I was a hero at Sarina, especially among other kids my age. Fancy scoring the winning try in men's A grade! Everyone agreed that it was a fantastic achievement, and for the first time I began to think that maybe I could go somewhere in league if I put my mind to it. For the past year or two people had been saying to me that I had so much potential I'd probably end up playing State of Origin for Queensland and that I might even play for Australia. It was nice to hear, but I don't think I took it seriously. Now, full of confidence after the A grade match, I began to think they might be right.

Two years later, at the age of 18, I was playing A grade for the Broncos against the best rugby league players in the world. Before that, in 1992, I made a Queensland Catholic schools team. I'm not a Catholic — I went to state schools right through from year one

— but I repeated my final year at St Patrick's College, a Catholic school in Mackay. The first full Queensland team I made was the under-19s. That was in 1993, which was also the year I made my first-grade debut for the Broncos. At the start of that year I trained for a week with the Broncos. Cyril Connell, the Broncos' recruitment manager, said to me, 'Mate, I want you to have a really good week. If you do, I'm pretty sure Wayne Bennett will offer you a contract.'

> 'Wendell hit me the hardest I've ever been hit. It stopped me dead, and I was hurt. It was the only tackle I haven't been able to stand up from.' Gorden Tallis, describing a tackle by young Wendell Sailor, who had recently joined the Broncos, in a match against St George, Tallis's team at the time.
>
> QUOTED BY **FRANK ROBSON** IN THE *GOOD WEEKEND*.

So I trained harder than I'd ever trained before, and I also won a 400-metre race against some of the fastest Broncos, including Willie Carne, who was a really good 400-metre runner. The trainer, Kelvin Giles, told me it was one of the best times any Bronco had run for the distance. Wayne called me in at the end of the week and said, 'Kelvin Giles reckons that if you're half as good a player as you are an athlete, you'll be pretty good.' He then looked at me and said, 'Can you play?' I replied, 'Yep, I can play.' Wayne said, 'Okay then, go ring your mother up. You've got two days to go home and pack your bags. I'm going to put you on a basic contract'.

I had come a long way quickly, and I give a lot of the credit for that to Mum and Dad. They were always supportive, they never knocked me, they never said, no, this or that can't be done. They always made me feel I was capable of anything, that there was nowhere I couldn't go, and this is how I approached life as I began climbing the ladder in league.

Pleasing my father and making him proud of me was one of my main motivations in getting to the top in football. I do know he was proud of me. He may have said so to me only a couple of times, but because he was a man of few words, a couple of times was enough. His favourite pastimes were fishing, watching league and, in particular, watching me. He liked to pull out old tapes of matches that I'd played in, maybe Origin 1996 or Origin 1998, and sit there by himself and watch them over and over.

The day my father died in 2001 was the hardest day of my life so far. We were so close that when he died I really felt part of me had died, too. I couldn't believe he had gone, and there hasn't been a day since that I haven't missed him. At the same time, Dad's death did have a positive effect on me. It made me realise that we should try to make the most of the time we have and appreciate the people who are close to us. My father was a very modest, unassuming type of person, and someone once asked me, 'How come your father's so humble and you're so arrogant?' I replied that arrogance had nothing to do with it. 'If you've seen your parents work so hard to get you to where you've got,' I said, 'you make sure you make the most of it. And you also make sure that you stay true to the person that your parents made you, that you don't try to be someone else'.

Dad was only 57 when he died. The cause of death was a heart attack, although as far as I know he'd never had heart trouble before. I do know his health hadn't been good, though, which was why he had retired from work a year earlier. By then, he had been working as a labourer for 29 years straight. Before Dad died, I had made up my mind to get him to as many of my union matches as I could. I planned to bring him down to Brisbane whenever I played for the Reds at Ballymore, and I had decided that if I was ever lucky enough to make the Wallabies I would fly him to every match, no matter where it was played — in New Zealand, South Africa or wherever. Sadly for me, I was never able to do this for him, but after he died I decided I would at least dedicate the rest of my career to him.

Dad was the third person very close to me I had lost in the space of six years. My sister, Michelle, died in 1996 of kidney and liver disease. She was only in her mid-30s, which made the tragedy all the harder to bear. Michelle had been flown to Brisbane and was in the Mater Hospital. Mum told me she was seriously ill and might not pull through, but I found this impossible to believe, and I told my mother so. A few days later, on a Sunday, I was training with the Broncos when a call came through from my mother. She told me to get to the hospital as soon as I could, because they were afraid Michelle was slipping away. By the time I arrived, Michelle had died. I went in and saw my mother bending over her, saying, 'She was too young — it should have been me.'

Michelle and I had never been close, because she had left home to go to Sydney when I was still young, but there was a strong bond between us, and her death left me reeling. I just couldn't believe someone as young and full of life as her could die. She was buried in Sarina on a Thursday, and the Broncos played Wests on the Friday night. Wayne Bennett offered to let me stand down for the match, but I insisted on playing, which was probably a mistake. I played one of my worst-ever games, dropping the ball three times in open space.

Then, in 1998, my best mate, Chris Felingham, died in a car accident. He was driving back to Sarina from Mackay with a friend one night, and their car hit a cane train. We had been best mates since primary school, and his death affected me as much as if he had been my brother. In some ways, Chris and I were complete opposites. He was fair-haired and blue-eyed — a pretty boy, as I used to call him. We had one thing in common — we were both attention-seekers — and to begin with we clashed because of this. By grade seven, though, we were best mates, and we stayed best mates until the end. Chris was a chef, and we shared a house soon after I came down to Brisbane. I have always thought that having my best mate from home with me really helped me cope with those first few years of playing with the Broncos.

I was godfather to Chris's daughter, and he was to be godfather to my son, Tristan. As it turned out, he never got to see Tristan. In 1998 he'd made a trip back to Queensland from Melbourne, where he was working as a chef, and we arranged to meet at Sarina after the Broncos played the Cowboys at Townsville. Tara was up there, too, with Tristan, who was then a few months old, and I was looking forward to showing Tristan off to Chris. I was chatting to Alfie Langer and a few of the boys the night before the match when a call came through from Tara. She said to me, 'You're not going to believe this: Chris has just been killed in a car accident.'

I couldn't speak. I started to cry and couldn't stop. After that I felt angry with the world, and I was still angry when we played a match a few nights later. I nearly got into a fight that night with Ian Roberts, and the rumour was I'd said something to him about his being a homosexual. That was completely untrue. When the incident happened I didn't even know it was Ian. He came in to tackle me and, feeling steamed up, I pushed his head away. He said to me, 'Wendell, you're f___ed!' and I thought then that I really was in for it, because I knew he could fight. In fact Johnny Lewis, the boxing trainer, once said (before Anthony Mundine switched to boxing) that if any league player could make it as a fighter it would be Ian Roberts.

So I had my hands up, expecting to cop a big one, when Gordy Tallis, who's pretty tough, too, came in to break it up. He said to Ian, 'Just f___ off and leave him (meaning me) alone.' Ian was still dirty at me, and whenever he tackled me again that match he'd say to me, 'Come on — how about throwing a punch?' I ignored him, so nothing happened, and after the match he came to me and said, 'Sorry for carrying on like that, mate,' and I said, 'Mate, I'm sorry for what I did, too.' That was the end of it.

We buried Chris at Mackay, and I was one of the pallbearers. More than four years later I still haven't got over losing him. I don't think I ever will.

NOT A QUESTION
OF COLOUR

Sarina was a smallish town — just under 4000 people — and for a boy growing up in a country town as small as that, there wasn't a lot to do apart from playing sport. This suited me, because I was good at sport and enjoyed playing it more than anything. The other thing was that people tended to think better of you if you played sport. Provided I was playing sport, nobody could say I was another black kid waiting for an opportunity to get into trouble. Sarina wasn't a racist town, but there were people who would have thought this way about me if I'd just hung around doing nothing.

I grew up well aware that people with an indigenous background, like me, had a tarnished reputation. They tended to be looked upon as people who just lay around, spent all their money on drink and got into fights. A few of my cousins and friends were like this: on the drink and making excuses for why they couldn't get a job. I never held this against them. Each of them must have had his own reasons for living the way he did, so who was I to judge? I just didn't want to be like that myself, especially since at that time I had ambitions of becoming a policeman.

Cathy Freeman was at Colonial Stadium in 2002 when I played my first rugby union Test. She said hello to me and afterwards she and her husband had a few drinks with us. Cathy and I have a lot in common. We're the same vintage and we come from the same part of the world. Also, we're both black. Cathy has had a fair bit to say over the years about Aboriginal issues and racism. So has Tony Mundine. I have a lot of respect for both of them. I'm quite aware of my colour. I'm aware of where I came from, but I have never wanted to push that line myself. I'm proud of my heritage, but I have no desire to identify myself with it.

Also, I have never, ever, wanted to use my heritage as an excuse for failure. What good does it do black Australians if we keep blaming other people for what's wrong with our lives? What good is it if we keep saying we're getting a raw deal because we're the victims of racism? There is racism in Australia — I know that as well as anybody, having been in the public eye since I was a teenager. But I also know there's less racism here than in just about every other country I can think of. People sometimes say to me I'm a great role model for black kids, but that's not what I want to be. I would like to be a role model for all Australian kids: black, white, brown, brindle. I certainly don't want to teach my son that he must have a particular loyalty to a particular skin colour.

The way forward for indigenous people is to be more positive and less negative. This was my father's attitude, and he was my role model all the time I was growing up. Dad was never out of work, he earned every dollar that he spent, he drank very little and he went out of his way to avoid any kind of trouble. In fact, for long periods he drank nothing at all. His attitude must have been bred into me. It was mainly for Dad's sake that I promised at the age of 15 never to have a drink until I had made it in football, which for me meant playing for Australia. It was also for my own sake. I knew what people thought about young blacks on the grog, and I didn't want to be thought of like that. By the age of 15, a lot of the kids I knew, both black and white, were already into the booze. I saw them around beach bonfires, smashing themselves on West Coast Coolers. I saw girls throwing up, and I saw my mates lying around, unconscious. It was not a great sight.

I kept that promise to my father. I did not drink until I was 21, and by that time I was well established as a first-grader with the Broncos. I had made my debut for Australia a year earlier. I had my first drink in six years at a party the Broncos boys put on for me when I turned 21. A big area was set aside at a Brisbane nightclub called City Rowers, and Fourex, one of the Broncos' main sponsors, laid on more than enough beer for everyone.

Until I went to the party I hadn't decided to 'break my drought', but that night I was under pressure from my Broncos mates to have a drink. Especially from Alfie Langer, who'd always been a supporter of mine at the Broncos and who was someone I looked up to. He said to me, 'Come on — you've got to have a drink at your own party.' So I did, knowing I'd already delivered on the promise to my father. I drank Sub Zeros with raspberry until five o'clock in the morning, and I ended up with the worst hangover. We'd played Cronulla in Brisbane that day before the party, and a few of the Cronulla players came along, too. Even today, when I meet those Cronulla boys they still say, 'How good was your party!'

I was proud a few years ago to be voted a place in an all-time Australian black league team, but, at the same time, I don't want to be typecast as black. Artie Beetson is the same. He is well aware of his Aboriginality, but you don't hear Artie talking about racial issues all the time. Likewise, I can't go along with the black footballers in rugby league, Aussie Rules or whatever code who complain about being the victims of racist abuse on the field. I've copped my share of racist insults on the field over the years, but I always saw this as part of the game, and gave as good as I got. If someone calls me a black prick, I'll call him a white prick back. But that's in the heat of the moment, and that's where it ends. The fact that an opposition player calls me a black prick doesn't mean he's a racist, that he has anything against black people, just as calling someone a fat prick doesn't mean you have anything against fat people. What the opposition player is doing is trying to sledge me, and, whether I like it or not, sledging is part of the game.

I don't condone racism, real racism, but I believe black sports-people can get paranoid about the subject. To run off and com-plain whenever you cop a racist insult on the field doesn't do you any good, the sport any good or, in my opinion, the cause of black people any good. This isn't to say that there's no racism out there, both off the football field and on it. I'm conscious of it all the time. A few years ago I was pulled over by a policeman in Brisbane while I was driving a new BMW that I'd bought not long after Super League began. The policeman came up to the car, recognised me and was apologetic, explaining that he'd pulled me over because he thought I didn't have a seatbelt on. In fact, I think one reason he pulled me over was that he saw a black guy driving an expensive car and thought that needed investigating. The same thing happened to Steve Renouf a year or two earlier.

My football trips to South Africa opened my eyes to what real racism is. George Gregan and I used to talk about it when we were there in 2002. George felt as deeply about it as I did, although it's not something he would want to talk about in public. I know South Africa has come a long way since the days of apartheid — and it has come a long way since my first visit in 1993 — but blacks still do all the crap jobs and generally have a lousy existence. Go to breakfast at a hotel in Australia and you'll be served by whites, browns, blacks — whoever happens to be on duty that morning. Go to breakfast in South Africa and you'll never be served by a white. Blacks do all the serving, all the bag-carrying.

Seeing all this got to me. On one of my first nights in South Africa with the Reds, I came across a black woman with two children begging in a Johannesburg shopping centre. One of her children was about three, the other was a baby in her arms. The woman had a sign in front of her saying, 'Please help — my children need food.' I gave her money, realising at the time that she might well have been a professional beggar and didn't deserve any. The inequality you see there is so bad that you feel you have to make some gesture, even one as small as this.

I had the feeling that there are still rednecks among South African whites, and I wouldn't be surprised if quite a few of them were at Ellis Park when the Wallabies played there in 2002. As I said to my mother after my earlier trip there with the Reds, an Australian who has never been to South Africa cannot know what real racism is. The situation in South Africa can't change quickly — new generations will have to replace old generations — but 25 years from now, when my son Tristan is about my age, I like to think he could go to South Africa and not find a trace of racism.

While there are definitely some real racists out there in Australia, and there are probably some real racists playing football, in my experience they're pretty rare. I feel that the more people talk about racism in Australia, the more they look for issues, the worse off indigenous Australians are. Instead of saying they deserve this or deserve that, Aborigines would be better off getting out and working for what they want in life. Black people in Australia have to look forward. If they keep trying to drag up the past, they will find themselves left behind in the past.

IN AT THE DEEP END

I began my new career in union running on from the bench for the Reds against the Waratahs. It was 6 October 2001, a Saturday. It's a day I won't forget. I'd played in the league preliminary final two Sundays earlier, and for the rest of that week I did a lot of drinking with my Bronco mates and other league people, who came to farewell me and wish me well. Then on the next Monday I got a call from the Reds, asking me to come in and talk about playing in the match against the Waratahs that Saturday. The idea of making my debut for the Reds so soon took me by surprise. After all, I'd been playing league for the Broncos until eight days earlier, and I still didn't know much about the basics of union, much less the finer points. Also, I'd just spent the best part of a week having farewell drinks — not the best preparation.

I drove to Ballymore and was introduced to the Reds' coach, Mark McBain, someone I hadn't met before. Mark said, 'Look, if you're keen to play this week we'll put you on the bench and give you 25 or 30 minutes in the game. On the other hand, if you don't think you're ready, that's okay, too — it's entirely up to you.' I said straight away, 'Yes, for sure. I'd love to play. Count me in.' The truth was I really wanted to play. Obviously, I was risking my reputation and could easily make a fool of myself, but that didn't worry me too much. I was just keen to get going with my new career.

> There was only one discussion point following the Centenary of Federation match against NSW. It didn't really matter that the Reds had won comfortably and that 16 Wallabies were running around. What mattered was that Sailor had taken the plunge, turning the final 25 minutes into a rugby pantomime. Everyone wanted to talk about Wendell's world. There was hilarity when the crowd chanted, 'Wendell, Wendell, Wendell', as he retrieved the ball for a Queensland penalty tap shortly after taking the field in the 55th minute.

GREG GROWDEN, REPORT IN THE *SYDNEY MORNING HERALD* ON SAILOR'S DEBUT MATCH FOR THE REDS AGAINST THE WARATAHS, OCTOBER 2001.

The media went berserk. Next morning the calls for interviews began at 6.30 and kept coming non-stop until mid-morning. They came not only from Queensland and NSW, as you would expect, but from media people all around Australia, from New Zealand, and even from London. What a week it was! Mark McBain gave me a crash course in union technique, teaching me the standard backline moves, how to lay the ball back and so on. Personally, I could have done without the media publicity. I would have liked to slip into the Queensland side and find my feet without a lot of fuss, but obviously that was never going to be possible. The one good thing about the publicity was that it attracted extra spectators. It was estimated afterwards that the fact that I would be playing drew an extra 6000 people. One of those extra spectators was my mother. She came down from Sarina to watch me. It was the first union match she had ever seen. It was also the first Tara had ever seen.

I was used to pressure. I'd played in plenty of big matches — grand finals, State of Origins, Tests, a World Cup final — before plenty of big crowds, and I'd never had much of a problem with nerves. But something about that debut match with the Reds got to me. I was more nervous on the day of the match than I had ever been in my entire football career. Tara hadn't seen me like it before. She asked, 'Are you all right?' My confidence should have been high after a good finals series with the Broncos, but on this day it was in tatters. On the rugby league field, everything was second nature to me. Now, I was about to run on to a rugby union field, unsure about what I should be doing or when I should be doing it, and knowing hardly any of the blokes in my own team. Also, I knew everyone would be watching everything I did.

I sat on the reserve bench during the first half, trying to compose myself. After half-time, I was given the signal and stood up to warm up. All of a sudden, without turning around, I realised that the crowd behind me was cheering me. I went on with my warm-up routine and the crowd kept cheering. I could tell from what they said that some of them were league fans. 'Show 'em how it's done, Wendell!' 'Give it to 'em, Sailor!' I thought at the time that this was like that famous scene at the MCG, where Merv

Hughes had the crowd going behind him while he was doing his stretches on the boundary.

I finally got on the field, with 25 minutes to go. There was a maul, and the first thing I did was clean out a bloke over the ball, which earned me a big cheer from the crowd. One of the other Reds — it might have been Fletcher Dyson — said to me, 'That's the first time I've ever heard anyone get cheered for cleaning someone out.' So far so good. Then we did a backline move named Bath, which involved me. It was one of 100 things I'd had to learn that week, but somehow I remembered it, and I knew what to do and where to be. The only trouble was that I didn't catch the ball when it was passed to me. I knocked on, and felt disgusted with myself. I couldn't remember when I last dropped a ball like that, and I couldn't believe I would do it here, the worst place possible. The amazing thing was that the crowd still cheered me. When I knocked on, they cheered!

I was more nervous than I'd ever been in my life on a football field, and apparently it showed. The Sydney rugby writer Greg Growden wrote that I was like 'a tongue-tied teenager at his first bush dance'. I played out the rest of the match without making any more mistakes, and I did manage to do some basic things successfully, like laying the ball back, so I felt fairly satisfied as I left the field. A couple of Queensland players — David Croft and Fletcher Dyson, I think — came up to me and congratulated me. They said they respected me for what I'd done that week. They also said they could see my public profile had helped promote the match. One of them said, 'You've got big balls and you've laid them on the line.' It was about the best compliment I'd ever received.

This was my first union match in Australia, and the difference between union and league was even greater than I had expected.

It wasn't just that the rules were different. Somehow, everything felt different. The atmosphere on the field was different in a way that's not easy to put into words. I wrote in an earlier chapter how different the crowds are at union and league matches. That's the thing Tara noticed at this match: how differently the spectators behaved. They reacted to things that happened on the field differently — applauding kicks, for example. Also, you didn't hear the same calls from the crowd, calls like 'F___ing get him' or 'Are you kidding yourself, Sailor?' or 'Wendell is a wanker', which had been chanted at me plenty of times.

Now I'm not suggesting that union spectators are all private-school silvertails who never say a word out of line, as a lot of league people still like to imagine. When it became known that I was switching to union, a few of my friends in league asked me in all seriousness how, as a working-class boy, I'd ever survive in union among all those well-educated snobs. That's what they honestly believed union followers were. My reply was that I didn't believe most union people were like that, but even if they were it wouldn't bother me, because I wasn't a bit ashamed of who I was or of coming from the background I came from. As it turned out, the social thing didn't even come up. Overall, union fans are as ordinary as anyone else, but the culture of their game is definitely different. Nobody can deny that.

Mark McBain was my first coach in rugby union, so he had a lot to do with how my career in union developed. The first thing he said to me was that he didn't want me to change my style of game. He wanted me to run with the ball in union just as I had run with it in league. He said the Reds would try to get the ball to me as much as possible, but he wanted me to go looking for it in certain situations and he specified the phases of play where this should happen.

They are not using Wendell as Wendell was used in rugby league, when the ball was thrown out to him on the wing and he was fairly destructive. When he was out wide there were very few occasions when he ran at someone one-on-one and was stopped. Without insulting the rugby union blokes, I think he [must be] be bored s___less.'

WALLY LEWIS, QUOTED BY ADAM HAWSE
IN THE *SUNDAY TELEGRAPH*, APRIL 2002.

Learning the backline moves was what I found hardest. It's not hard to beat a man or run into a hole. For me, anyway, the hard thing was to run the right lines — to make sure I was in the right place at the right time in the criss-cross moves, because I knew that a mistake here could be fatal. Backline moves in union are definitely more complicated than in league, and to run the wrong line when a move is on in union means you're letting the rest of the team down.

I was aware of this and felt under pressure because of it. I'd always had plenty of confidence on the football field, but when Queensland's Wallabies rejoined the Reds for training sessions after Christmas I felt a bit overawed. All of a sudden I was involved in backline moves with people like Daniel Herbert, Chris Latham and Ben Tune, and when I stuffed up with the drills, as I sometimes did, I felt a bit like the dumb kid at school who's holding the rest of the class back. I used to apologise to the others when I got it wrong, and they were always good about it. But learning the moves was a big problem for me, and I lost some sleep over it. For a while after New Year I wondered if I'd ever get the hang of it.

Macka, as we called Mark McBain, had lunch with Wayne Bennett and asked him what was the best way to coach me. Wayne's reply was, 'Just get the ball in his hands as much as you can.' For a few different reasons, things didn't work out that way. For the Reds, I had between 18 and 24 touches of the ball per game. For the Broncos, I used to have between 30 and 45. For the Reds I averaged about nine runs per game. For the Broncos, I averaged 19. In other words, I had the ball in my hands nearly twice as much. Playing for the Reds, I often felt I was wasted, but I know that's a common winger's complaint in union.

After a shaky start, Sailor impressed as the tournament wore on into last night's final against Australia and New Zealand. His contact work and positioning improved with every one of the five games he played from a possible six. And in the quarter-final against England, when he finally scored his first try, his feisty spirit – which once inspired the Broncos to so much success – even returned.

RUPERT GUINNESS, REPORT IN *THE AUSTRALIAN* ON SAILOR'S PERFORMANCE IN THE WORLD RUGBY SEVENS IN BRISBANE, FEBRUARY 2002.

In early February, a few weeks before Super 12 began, I played in the World Rugby Sevens at Ballymore. I couldn't believe the number of countries that took part. All the main rugby nations were there, plus teams from Japan, the United States, Canada, Papua New Guinea, even China. My picture was used big-time in the lead-up publicity, probably because they thought it would attract league fans — as well as union fans who were curious to see how I'd go. Jim Tucker wrote an article in the *Courier-Mail* in Brisbane, saying that players from other countries wondered who the black bloke was in the advertisements. They knew nothing about league, so they didn't have a clue who I was. Tucker quoted one of the French players saying, 'Who is he? I have never heard of him, so it is a surprise that he is the player on all the posters.' The Chinese captain said, 'Ah, he's the big black man. I've seen him on TV and around the hotel ... he looks very strong.'

I did okay. I scored a try in the quarter-final against England and another try in the semi against Samoa. Before the final against New Zealand, Rupert Guinness wrote in *The Australian*, 'After a shaky start, Sailor impressed as the tournament wore on ... His contact work and positioning improved with every one of the five games he played.' But Guinness thought Mat Rogers did better than me, and he quoted me agreeing with this. 'Mat is more of a brain,' I was quoted as saying. 'He knows where to be.'

The Sevens tournament ran for two days, and more than 20,000 people came to watch, which was a lot more than two years earlier when the same tournament was staged for the first time in Brisbane. People seemed to think that the fact that I was playing had a lot to do with the size of the crowds. Jim Tucker said in the *Courier-Mail* that even if I was on a $750,000 contract, as some journalists were suggesting, the ARU had got an absolute bargain. He wrote, 'Rugby's ruling body saved a packet over the past week. Why? Because every time a camera or microphone was pointed into the sky, it seemed Sailor came into focus to plug the Sevens.'

ONE OF THE REDS

What I feared more than anything when I signed to play union was that I might not get beyond club football. In other words, that I might not make the Queensland team. Willie Carne hadn't found it easy, and Willie, I knew, had been a great league winger. So the big hurdle for me was to be picked as one of the Reds. As the time for selections drew near, it seemed to me that this was far from certain. Ben Tune obviously had the right wing sewn up, and Ricky Nalatu was pushing me hard for the left wing. In the end I think I got in just ahead of him.

This is how it happened. I'd missed our trial match against the Crusaders at Christchurch because of a hamstring injury. I had to pull out two days before the match, which was frustrating for me, because at that time I needed every opportunity to make an impression on the selectors. Our next trial was against the Auckland Blues. There were two trial matches, between A sides and B sides; I was picked in the Reds' A team and Ricky Nalatu in the B. The A team played in Auckland, and while I made a few breaks and did a couple of good tackles, I felt I hadn't done anything to convince Mark McBain that I deserved the No.11 jersey. This was my first and last trial game, and we'd just been beaten by 40 points. I remember thinking to myself that, all in all, things had definitely not worked out as well as they could have. The newspaper report said I'd given a 'competent' performance — okay but not great. Ricky went all right, without doing anything outstanding.

I came home and began to worry. The team for the first Super 12 match, against the Brumbies, was about to be announced, and as I sat and thought about it I began to think I might not even make the 22. I would have been happy to sit on the bench for three or four matches while I learned the ropes, as Andrew Walker did when he joined the Brumbies. But I knew they hardly ever put wingers on the bench, and I could see that putting me in the starting XV would be a gamble. Since leaving the Broncos I'd played only one and a half matches of union, and Mark McBain would have been aware that I still didn't know all the moves. I had no idea what he thought of me. He was one of those poker-faced types who didn't give anything away.

There was a training session arranged at Ballymore for 10 am, but Anthony Herbert, the Reds' team manager, phoned to ask if I'd come in half an hour early. Fearing the worst, I said, 'Oh yeah — why's that?' Anthony said, 'Mate, there's a few blokes that Macka wants to speak to before the session.' For me, this was as good as saying I hadn't made the team. The only reason I could see that Macka would want to speak to me before training was to break the bad news to me and let me down gently. For the first time since I'd made the decision to switch to union, I was seriously looking at the possibility that I would turn out to be a dud.

The drive from my home at Mount Ommaney to Ballymore was the longest I'd ever done. I kept thinking of what the Broncos boys would be saying among themselves when they heard I hadn't been selected, 'How's this? He went over there to make it big-time and now he hasn't even got into the Queensland team.' Before I reached Ballymore I decided I had to shut all this out of my mind and think positive, but it wasn't easy. When I arrived I found there were maybe six or seven other players who'd come early to speak to Macka. The two halfbacks, Jacob Rauluni and Sam Cordingley, were there, and it was obvious from the way they looked that Jacob had just been given the nod over Sam. Ricky Nalatu and Junior Pelesasa, who was able to play wing, were there, too. My mind started racing: maybe it's Junior, not Ricky, who's going to be No.11. Maybe I'm only third in line for the position.

We waited to speak to Macka, one by one, in his room. I was one of the last to go in, and Ricky went in before me. I watched him as he came out. He had his head down and his body language wasn't good, but I wasn't sure if that meant anything. I said to him, 'How did you go, Ricky? Are you in?' By this time we'd all become pretty good mates. Ricky, in particular, had often helped me out, showing me what to do. He said to me, 'I think you're in, mate. Good luck.' So I went into the room. Mark McBain was sitting there with Anthony Herbert and the two assistant coaches, Roger Gould and Adrian Thompson. Macka said to me, 'We've looked at you closely, Wendell, and we like what we see. We think you'll be an asset to the team. You'll be starting next week against the Brumbies.'

I thought, 'Yes! Yes!' The relief I felt was tremendous, although I was careful not to show it. They had chosen me as No.11 and Junior as a utility back on the bench. Ricky wasn't in the team, and I felt truly sorry for him, because he really hadn't put a foot wrong and he could easily have been picked ahead of me. When I came out, feeling pumped, there were congratulations all round. I sensed the boys were genuinely pleased that I'd made it. At least I was getting a start. Now it was up to me to make sure I kept my place in the team.

He's already said he's had to learn more moves in this one week than he did in nine years of rugby league. It's just the nature of rugby. So much more is worked off set plays.

MATT COCKBAIN, SPEAKING TO THE MEDIA IN OCTOBER 2001 AFTER SAILOR BEGAN TRAINING WITH THE REDS.

From the first day I joined the Reds, Daniel Herbert went out of his way to help me settle in. He told me that if I ever wanted to discuss anything about the game with him, I should just give him a call. So he was the one I'd go to first if I needed to have something explained to me at training. The rest of the team was much the same: they did their best to make me feel at home. More than one of them advised me not to make too many changes to what I'd been doing in league, to keep running with the same power and footwork.

Chris Latham was a big help to me. He chatted to me about the game when I first arrived at the Reds, and he often gave me advice on the field, maybe telling me to move up 10 metres or come back 20. Off the field, I got on particularly well with the two halfbacks, Sam Cordingley and Jacob Rauluni.

Some of the blokes were quite different from what I expected. Ben Tune was one of these. On the field he plays with a lot of passion, but off the field he's a really quiet guy. Not long after joining the Reds I asked him if he was coming along to have a drink with the rest of us, and he said, 'No, the V8s are on.' I found he was a bloke who liked to spend his time at home watching the V8 Supercars.

For me, one of the down sides of going to union was having to listen to the stories the media kept running about how much I was being paid and whether or not I was worth it. It was something I could never get interested in — and I was the one the stories were about! Maybe the public was interested in the subject, but I found it a bore. The honest truth is that money isn't all that big a deal with me. Like everyone else, I enjoy having money, but it's way down my list of priorities. Andrew Johns once said that most league players would play for nothing if they had to, and I am sure this is true. For me, the football comes first and the money comes a distant second.

SUPER 12 DEBUT

The Reds' first Super 12 match of the season — my Super 12 debut — was against the Brumbies in Canberra. As I knew from experience in league, there are good and bad things to be said about playing another team from your own country. One is that everyone has a pretty good idea how every opposing player will perform. That day against the Brumbies — the date was 23 February 2002 — I could see that everybody knew everybody's game inside out. We knew before we ran on what Georgie Gregan was likely to do in any situation and what Stephen Larkham was likely to do. We also knew what we had to do to stop them, although doing it would obviously be another matter.

It's also a fact that when Australian teams play each other, whether in union or league, they're not just playing to win. They're also playing for a spot in the national side, and this means that the competition can get a bit fiercer than usual. Because this was the first round of the season, though, national selections seemed a long, long way ahead, and I don't think anyone on the field gave them much thought.

I know I didn't. There were too many other things on my mind. I was under a fair bit of personal pressure. There'd been a lot of hype in the media about Wendell Sailor switching to rugby union and what he might or might not do when he got there. I knew I had to look past that and realise that I just had to play to the best of my ability. At the same time, I also had to remember that it was a new game for me. Usually my confidence takes over when I'm on the field, but I knew I had to tread lightly when I started playing union. I had to make sure I avoided the obvious mistakes, such as getting turned over after being tackled. Basically, I did not want to be a hindrance to the team.

In league I'd earned the respect of the people who follow the sport and, what was more important, the respect of the players. In union, I didn't have that respect. It was as if I was starting all over again.

Before the match, one of the guys in the team said to me, 'Are you nervous?' I told him no. 'Well,' he said, 'we are' — meaning they were worried I might stuff things up. He was having a shot at me, but it was in fun. I think the other Reds knew — at least I hope they knew! — that I had too much pride, too much competitive spirit, too much ambition to do well, call it what you will, to let them down. In fact, just about every bloke in the team had been wishing me well all week before the match, which shows how wrong a few of my league mates had been when they warned me that I'd probably get a frosty reception from the union boys. They'd said that some union players would resent all the publicity I was getting and maybe even hope that I messed up.

What do I remember about that first Super 12 match? I do remember that the ACT crowd gave me a hard time, although this did not put me off. That type of thing never does. Throughout the whole of my career, I seem to have been one of those players that opposition fans love to hate. I've always been confident on the field, and maybe they see that as arrogance. Whatever the reason, being jeered at and cat-called by the opposition crowd has never bothered me. On the contrary: I thrive on it. It gets me wound up.

In any case, I expected that the ACT crowd would give it to me. Canberra crowds always have. In fact, whenever I've crossed the Queensland border, crowds have given it to me. That didn't worry me: I was a Queenslander, a Bronco, so I expected it. When the crowd in Sydney chanted 'Wendell is a wanker' at the State of Origin matches, I took it as a compliment, knowing they obviously saw me as a threat.

> *He switched codes to strut his stuff on a more global stage and the world is now watching. His reputation won't carry the same intimidation factor it did in league, simply because he hasn't got one among so many opponents.*
>
> **JIM TUCKER.** PREVIEW IN THE *COURIER-MAIL* OF THE WORLD RUGBY SEVENS IN BRISBANE. FEBRUARY 2002.

Wayne Bennett set me straight on that before one Origin match in Sydney. I happened to mention that I was expecting to cop it again from the Sydney crowd, and he said, 'You know why they do that? Because you're now a presence on the field, you've got a reputation. They know you're a player that can turn the match against them.' I should add that Brisbane crowds do the same thing in reverse. They always gave Laurie Daley plenty in the Origin matches there. They also did a similar sort of chant: 'Freddy is a wanker, Freddy is a wanker.' (For those who don't know, Freddy is Brad Fittler's nickname.)

Sometimes I copped more than chants and insults. At Wollongong, when I played there a few years ago, some spectators threw bottles at me. I was having a good game and the crowd started to have a go at me, which, as always, pumped me up even more. The more they bagged me, the more I swaggered, which I often do to rile the crowd. It all came to a head when somebody cross-kicked and I ran 90 metres to score. As I walked back, deliberately looking pleased with myself, the crowd really got into me, shouting everything they could think of at me. I turned to where most of the noise was coming from and laughed at them. This was more than they could take. The next thing I knew I was being pelted with bottles and bits of rubbish, none of which, luckily for me, connected.

Wayne Bennett made a statement after this incident, saying how shocking it was that a crowd would behave that way, that this was something he'd hoped he'd never see at any rugby league ground in Australia. A player of Wendell Sailor's standing deserved respect, he said, even from the opposition. A few days later, though, he took me aside and asked, 'Del, did you stir that crowd up?' I said, 'Well, they gave it to me and I gave it to them.' He said, 'You know I stuck up for you afterwards.' I replied that I appreciated that, and I assured him that I'd done nothing wrong. All I'd done, really, was play with a lot of passion, which got under the crowd's skin.

I also had trouble with the crowd in 2000 when we went down to play Canterbury-Bankstown. I had a quiet first half, but in the second half I scored two tries and set up a third. It was a multicultural crowd and their blood was up. They'd been having a go at me in the usual way, calling out, 'Wendell is a wanker', and after I scored a 50-metre try I held my fingers to my lips and went, 'Shhhhh', as if I was telling them that they should now be quiet. Darren Smith, one of my best mates in the Broncos, saw what I was doing and said, 'Wendell, just don't do that, mate.' He obviously thought I was stirring up the crowd too much. I said to him, 'No, I couldn't give a stuff about them.' Wayne Bennett thought I was stirring up the crowd too much, too, and later had a go at me because of it.

But to get back to the Brumbies' match: nothing the ACT spectators shouted at me that day worried me in the slightest, because I'd experienced much worse before. It wouldn't have worried me, either, if the Brumbies players had had a shot at me, too, but this didn't happen. In fact, the Brumbies did not say a thing to me. This was a surprise, because I'd been warned by a few people that I could expect a verbal bashing. Even one of the Brumbies — Peter Ryan, my old Bronco team-mate, who'd been to my wedding a few months earlier — thought I was in for it. He phoned me a few days before the match to congratulate me on making the starting line-up. Peter was a good mate, and a few months earlier he'd come to my wedding. He said, 'Mate, if you get caught on the wrong side of the ruck you know I'm going to give it to you.' I wished him luck but said he'd have to catch me first, to which he replied that there'd be no problem catching me — I'd never see him coming.

He gave me another warning: 'A few of the Brumbies boys are good sledgers, so you'd better watch out.' When I asked him which Brumbies he was talking about, he said George Gregan was a good sledger and so was Owen Finegan. He said, 'Mate, the boys will probably sledge you a bit. I thanked him for the tip but told him that wouldn't bother me at all. 'Well, that's fine, Wendell', he said. 'Just go out and do what you do, play the way you normally play — and good luck!' But on the day I got no sledges at all.

Even when Georgie Gregan knocked the ball out of my hands, nothing was said to me. If something had been said to me then, I couldn't have felt worse than I did. What happened was that George stripped the ball from me about two metres from the line. I'd just beaten Andrew Walker inside and I saw George coming across, but I didn't think there was any way he'd stop me because I was so close to the line. I could have dived for the line there and then and been guaranteed a try, but I kept running because I wanted to ground the ball close to the posts. Suddenly, from nowhere, Gregan got to me and stripped the ball from my hands. I expected him to try to tackle me like he did Jeff Wilson back in that Bledisloe Cup match back in 1994, and I was sure he couldn't do that. I never expected him to try to strip the ball from me and I still don't know how he did it — it had never happened to me before. 'Where the hell did that go?', I thought to myself.

I was mad at myself afterwards because I love scoring tries, and this try was there for the taking. If I'd scored it, it would have given my Super 12 career a dream start. I was still fuming about it when somebody put up a box kick. As I was getting under it I took a peek at the bloke coming at me and I juggled it. As he hit me I went to retrieve it, but I fumbled it again and the ball went loose and was picked up by George Gregan, who passed it to someone. I was filthy at myself before, but I was much filthier at myself now.

This is what I had to say in my column in the *Courier-Mail* a few days later: 'Just because I'm playing rugby doesn't mean the old advice of my Broncos' mentor, Wayne Bennett, has lost its value. He always reckoned one of my worst traits is getting caught in two minds. "Don't slow down the process by too much thinking ... just get the ball and run," Benny would keep saying. In Canberra [against the Brumbies], I was thinking about keeping the ball out in front if I needed to pass, which gave George Gregan his chance to fleece me. Right again, Benny.'

Having the ball knocked out of my hands was a pity for me, but it proved again that really top players like Gregan are able to produce a turning point in the match. This was certainly a turning point, because if I'd scored we would have been only two points behind the Brumbies.

So my first appearance in Super 12 wasn't as successful as it might have been. On the other hand, I wasn't shown up for my lack of experience in union — I didn't commit any of the blunders you might expect of someone new to the game — which was something to be thankful for. I had one other thing to be thankful for: the support that I received before the match from my mates in league. A few of them were in Canberra to watch me make my Super 12 debut against the Brumbies. Jason Croker, a good mate of mine on the league World Cup trip in 2000, was one of them. He said, 'Mate, what about you just doing push-ups out on the wing unless they give you the ball more?' I said, 'It's different from league, mate — you've got to understand. The mentality of the codes is different. That's why Garrick Morgan came across and didn't make it in league.'

Quite a few others had phoned me before the match. Laurie Daley called to wish me all the best, which I really appreciated. 'I know you'll do well,' he said. Even though we'd always been opponents on the field, Laurie had been ready at all times to give me a helping hand. When I first came into the game he took me aside and gave me some tips. One of them, I remember, was to be myself, to play my own game. His support continued after I switched to union, and I was very appreciative of that.

Andrew Johns gave me a good-luck call, too, and so did Trent Barrett. And, of course, I had plenty of calls from my old mates at the Broncos. Gorden Tallis, Darren Lockyer and Lote Tuqiri were three I remember phoning, and I also had a call from Wayne Bennett, who wished me all the best and quizzed me about how I was making the adjustment to union. I had many other calls before and after that from league players who were interested to hear first-hand how I was going, what union was like and, in particular, how different the training was. I told them that the training we did in union was much more structured than in league, where you tend to do a lot more things ad lib.

SIN-BINNED

I believe sledging is part of the game, as long as it's done one on one. I used to be a fairly big sledger in rugby league, probably because I felt completely confident about my own ability. Wayne Bennett once said to me that talking to the opposition on the field is fine as long as you can back up the words with action. Alfie Langer, who with Wayne Bennett is right up there at the top of the list of people I respect in rugby league, said much the same thing to me one day. 'You might be a lair on the field and do a lot of talking,' Alfie said, 'but I appreciate the fact that you back it up.'

So in league I had a reputation for being pretty good at sledging and nearly always giving better than I got. My standard tactic was to tell the player I was sledging that he was a nobody, so nothing he said was worth anything. So if someone said, 'Sailor, you're not even that good', I might say, 'Who are you? What have you done in your life? You're a nothing.' But if you're going to take this line when you sledge, you have to have the performances on the field to back it up. Which is why I found myself in a different position when I crossed over to union.

Before my first game with the Reds — against the Waratahs in October 2001 — I was warned that a few of the Waratahs would probably have a go at me, and I was told that if anyone was going to sledge me it would probably be Tom Bowman. I was also warned to make sure I never ended up on the wrong side of the ruck because the Waratahs would be sure to ruck my insides out. I knew getting rucked out was no fun. Just a day or two earlier Roger Gould told me how he'd had to have an ear sewn back together after he got rucked in the head during a Test. So I was ready for the worst when I ran out from the bench in the second half, but nothing happened. I wasn't sledged by Tom Bowman or anyone else. Nothing was said to me by the Waratahs at all.

The former Brisbane Broncos' winger may not have known that the Chinese or Cook Islanders even played rugby before this event, but he's always known the English jumper as a red rag in any sport. So it proved when Sailor deliberately created a personal duel with strapping former English Test winger Leon Lloyd to fire up his tournament ... Richard Graham [the Australian captain] even feared Sailor might cop a yellow card for being over-aggressive and too verbal with Lloyd.

JIM TUCKER, WRITING IN THE *COURIER-MAIL* ABOUT THE WORLD RUGBY SEVENS IN BRISBANE, FEBRUARY 2002.

Future Wallaby: Wendell in a sailor suit
(Sailor Family collection)

Too small to reach the pedals
(Sailor Family collection)

Straw hat, bare feet
(Sailor Family collection)

Wendell in long pants, posing
(Sailor Family collection)

Wendell, a mate and a boot full of mangoes
(Sailor Family collection)

Junior cricketer. Wendell (at rear) was playing for Central Queensland
(*Sailor Family collection*)

Mackay under-12 footballer, 1986. His team was North Queensland champion
that year (*Sailor Family collection*)

Player of promise... Wendell in 1992, before he moved to Brisbane
(*Sailor Family collection*)

Wendell around the time he joined the Broncos
(*Sailor Family collection*)

Sailor with his No.1 fan – his father, Daniel
(*Sailor Family collection*)

Wendell and his parents. This photo was taken in 2000, the year
before his father's death (*Sailor Family collection*)

The Sailor family:
Tara, Tristan and Wendell
(Sailor Family collection)

At home with wife Tara and son Tristan
(Sailor Family collection)

Nothing but happiness on Tara and Wendell's wedding day
(*Geoff Letchford*)

Premiers again. Sailor and Brad Thorn raise the trophy for the Broncos in 2000
(Chris Lane/Action Photographics)

Sailor soars for the ball – and wins it for the Broncos. Contrary to some media suggestions, Sailor has a sound record under the high ball
(*Daniel Berehulak/Action Photographics*)

Sailor scores in the corner for the Broncos against North Queensland
(*Colin Whelan/Action Photographics*)

At the league World Cup final in 2000, Sailor fights to prevent New Zealander
Stephen Kearney driving him over the line
(*AP Photo/Max Nash/AAP Image*)

Father and son. Tristan Sailor hopes to follow his father's lead and play for the Broncos, Kangaroos, Reds and Wallabies – in that order
(*Daniel Berehulak/Action Photographics*)

The Broncos have won again: time for a rest
(Colin Whelan/Action Photographics)

In full stride for the Broncos
(*Sailor Family collection*)

Sailor's popularity with Broncos fans meant he was sorely missed when he crossed to rugby union *(Chris Lane/Action Photographics)*

Bronco star
(Colin Whelan/Action Photographics)

Sailor leaves the field in a Bronco's jersey for the last time – at the end of the preliminary final against Parramatta at Stadium Australia in 2001. He later wept with emotion while farewelling team-mates *(Daniel Berehulak/Action Photographics)*

Sailor back at hard training on the day his move to rugby union was announced *(AAP Image/Dave Hunt)*

My next appearance was for Australia in an international Sevens tournament at Ballymore. This time there was the usual sledging between players. I copped a bit, and I gave a bit, too. In particular, I remember having a pretty lively exchange with an England winger. We went on to make the final, where we beat New Zealand to win the tournament. New Zealand didn't have a lot of big-name All Blacks, but they did have some good Sevens players. I got caught with the ball, trying to get around one of the New Zealanders who managed to grab my jersey. He said to me, 'Sailor, you're no good. They ought to get another player on instead of you.' I came back with, 'Who are you? What's your name? Can somebody get me a program, because I don't even know this bloke's name.' Someone else in the team who heard it must have thought it was a good line because some time later I saw it quoted in a newspaper.

One or two of the Reds quizzed me about it. They asked, 'Do you sit at home working out things to say or do they just pop out?' They do pop out. I've been saying things on the field like that for as long as I've been playing. Before our match against the Hurricanes, Daniel Herbert said, 'Wendell, if you get into a tangle with Jonah Lomu, don't ask him who he is. You're supposed to know.'

Sledging is one thing. Fighting is another. I have never condoned fighting on the field. It may excite some spectators at the time and give the television commentators something to talk about, but overall it's bad for the game. I think the players involved in it always end up looking pretty stupid, and if you get sin-binned for fighting it could cost your team the game. But no matter how hard you try to avoid it, sometimes you can get caught up in a situation.

In the second Super 12 match of the season, against the Auckland Blues in Brisbane, I had a run-in with Ron Cribb, who's been an All Blacks backrower. I'd half-bumped him during the play, and he grabbed my jersey and pushed me back and I grabbed his and pushed him back. We're standing there, holding jerseys, and he said, 'Come on, then,' and I said, 'Why don't you come on?' It was all pretty silly: we could have been two boys in the schoolyard. I did manage to finish off with a slightly better line. He had buffed-up hair, so I called him Soulglo, which was the name of a hair gel in an Eddie Murphy movie. He said again that he'd take me on, and I said, 'Sure, Soulglo. I'm number 11. That's my number — you can find me any time. I'll be here all day.' After a bit more eye contact, that's where we left it.

A week later, playing against the Waikato Chiefs at Brisbane, I got caught up in another scuffle. This one was a lot more serious, because the other guy and I both got sent off. The other guy was a big second-rower called Keith Robinson. I'd never played against him before, of course, and, to be honest, I don't think I'd ever heard of him until that day. It all began with a fairly small incident which happened, I think, in the first 10 minutes of the match. I was off the ball, and Robinson went out of his way to push me, grabbing my jersey and trying to shove me to one side. I said to him, 'What do you think you're doing, you idiot?' He looked at me and said, 'Do you want a go?' I just walked away.

In the second half there was another incident, and it was this that brought everything to a head. I was in much the same position, standing off the ball. Robinson went out of his way to have a go at me again, and this time I got really filthy. For a fraction of a second I felt the way a kid feels before a fight in the playground at school. You're busting to hit the other bloke, but at the same time you know you mustn't hit him because it will get you into trouble. This time I couldn't help myself: I went at him, throwing punches. He back-pedalled, but being a bloke nearly two metres tall he had the reach to keep me at bay. I kept coming at him, throwing punches, but he kept going backwards and my punches kept just missing. In fact, none of the punches I threw connected, and none of his connected, either, which was probably a good thing for both of us.

So we were sent off for 10 minutes. I was really stirred up at this stage, and when I saw a few of the Waikato boys looking at me I let fly at them, too, saying something like: 'Who the f___ are you looking at?' As Robinson and I left the field we kept sledging each other. Even off the field we exchanged some words, and as I was warming up to go back on I looked at him and laughed, which made him mad at me again.

We shook hands, but he wasn't very friendly. After a flare-up like that, I'm usually one to forgive and forget, but he was still pretty cranky, and that was probably because of the way I'd sledged him when we were leaving the field. I gave him an earful, telling him he was a nobody, that he knew nothing, that he'd done nothing and so on. He came back, suggesting we finish it after the match, which I thought was pretty silly. In my opinion, he had obviously gone out of his way to intimidate me. The boys gave me heaps about it afterwards. We all had a laugh about it in the dressing room, and maybe Keith Robinson had a laugh about it later, too. I hope so, because I certainly don't hold any grudge against him.

In another way, though, the whole thing wasn't a bit funny. The fact that I was off the field for 10 minutes meant I had let my team down. To be honest, I wasn't proud of my part in the affair.

Being sent off isn't my style. In nine years with the Broncos I was sent off only once. It was in a match against St George–Illawarra at WIN Stadium in 1999 or maybe 2000. Darren Smith, one of my best mates at the Broncos, was at dummy half, and I turned around to see the marker laying into him, so I grabbed the marker and began laying into him. The touch judge reported that I had come from 10 metres away to throw punches, so the ref sent me off. In fact, I was about one metre away.

I could have been sent off in 2001, too, but for some reason the ref decided against it. Darren Treacy of St George had been niggling me, and I got into a scuffle with him after he pushed me in the face as he was playing the ball. I threw a few punches, and I think the ref saw it, but all he did was award a penalty. As I said before, I don't agree with fighting on the field, and if you do it you can't complain if you get sin-binned. On that day I was just dead lucky.

Mark McBain had warned me before the Super 12 season started that I would probably get baited a lot. Someone asked me later if I thought Robinson had been given the job of having a go at me as part of a team plan to upset me and put me off my game. Maybe this is what happened, but I doubt it. I think he did it off his own bat, although I have no idea why. I do know that some opposition players resented the fact that I'd been getting a lot of publicity and had decided that I needed to be cut down to size. Even in New Zealand my transfer to union had a lot of media exposure, and maybe some of the boys there wanted to take some of the shine off me. If so, that was bad luck for me.

THE LONG WAIT
FOR A TRY

After my first few Super 12 matches I began to feel I really belonged with the Reds, and I began to feel at home at Ballymore. The important thing was that I had kept my place in the team. I made the odd mistake in those first few games, none of them too costly, but I also made some good driving runs. My goal was to make sure in each match that I performed better than I had in the previous one.

A group of my former Bronco mates began following the Reds to watch me play. Gorden Tallis was one of them. After watching my first few Super 12 games he said, 'You're not getting enough ball out there. How can you score a try?' I said, 'It'll come, Gordy, it'll come.' I didn't realise then just how long it would take to come.

I was surprised at how many league people generally made a point of watching me play — people who had hardly ever watched union before. Tara's father, Dennis 'Hockey' Vernon, was a diehard league follower, just like my own father, but as soon as I started playing Super 12 he became a fan of the Reds and began watching all the union he could. He soon got to know all the rules, and he even took to watching the television program

Inside Rugby. I'd like to think that my father would have been the same, that he would have got interested in union once he began watching me play, but of course he didn't live long enough for that. Even so, I knew league would always have been his first love. In fact, on the day he died he was watching NRL on pay-TV.

One of the things that kept me going during those first few weeks of Super 12 was the support of my Queensland team-mates and our coach, Mark McBain. They kept telling me I was playing well, that I was on the right track, that I should keep going. If I hadn't had that kind of feedback, that kind of support, I could easily have lost confidence. At training, McBain got me to focus on breakdown work — I think with good results. I can remember only a few occasions in all the Super 12 matches I played in 2002 when the ball was lost after I was tackled.

In the first couple of Super 12 matches I had a problem with the high ball. It happened once with a box kick in the very first match of the Super 12 season. It happened again in the second match, against the Auckland Blues, also with a box kick. As the kick went up I decided it was mine and moved in to get under it, but just as I was about to go up for the ball our halfback, Jacob Rauluni, called for it. I half pulled out and left it to Jacob, who dropped it. On the strength of this, word went around in the media that I was suspect under the high ball, which really annoyed me, because it wasn't true.

Actually, this wasn't the first time I'd been accused of being suspect under the high ball. It had happened once before, after I dropped two high balls in the State of Origin match in 1998. I was filthy with myself for doing it, but everyone drops high balls occasionally, and it just happened that I dropped two in a game that everyone was watching. But over the whole of my career I haven't dropped many, and I know for a fact that it's not a weakness of mine. If I was suspect under the high ball I'd admit it, but it just isn't true. I felt it was another case of the media wanting to tag people with something — he can't kick, he can't catch, he can't tackle or whatever. I often heard it said that David Campese was suspect in front-on defence. I watched a fair bit of Campese on television, but I can't honestly remember him ever missing a front-on tackle. Maybe he missed them when I wasn't watching. Or maybe he was tagged unfairly by the media, too.

But all the talk about me being suspect under the high ball was nothing compared with the talk about me not scoring a Super 12 try. In fact, this became one of the great talking points of the Super 12 season. Union fans kept asking, 'When will Sailor finally make it across the line?' and as match after match went by and I still hadn't done it they asked the question more and more. People wondered how it was possible that someone who had scored so many tries as a league player would struggle to score even one in an equivalent competition in union. Was it that defence in union was a lot tougher than anyone realised? Was it that I was running the wrong lines? Or was it that I just wasn't getting enough ball?

The media weren't slow to pick up on this last point. When I hadn't scored a try in the first three or four matches, journalists began phoning me and asking whether I thought I might have scored seven or eight tries by now if I'd been playing for the Brumbies instead. The suggestion was that because of the way the Reds played I wasn't seeing enough ball. It was true I wasn't getting nearly as much ball as I did with the Broncos, but it really wasn't fair to compare the Reds with the Broncos like that. After all, they were two different codes.

One journalist asked me straight out if I thought I'd made a mistake choosing to play for the Reds. 'If you'd been at the end of the Brumbies' backline,' he said, 'you probably would have scored six or seven tries by now.' I didn't rise to the bait. I simply said that I was happy playing with the Reds and that, tries or no tries, my rugby union career was still on track. The journalist kept at it. 'Even if you'd been playing with the Waratahs,' he said, 'you'd probably have scored four or five tries.' I replied, 'If you're looking for an angle you'd better look elsewhere. You won't get it from me.'

So I kept up a brave face, but inside I was feeling pretty frustrated. The fact that I should have scored a try in my very first Super 12 game didn't help. In league, I had made my reputation scoring tries. In eight years with the Broncos I'd scored 110 of them. I wasn't living up to that reputation in union. I've always performed best with the ball in hand when I've had a bit of space, but somehow I did not often find myself in this position in the Super 12 matches. I'd made some good breaks, and I'd created opportunities for others, but somehow the tries kept eluding me. My general play was sound. My defence was as good as ever — I wasn't losing the ball in tackles — and most of the time I was turning up at the right place and time in the backline moves. But still no try! Meanwhile, Ben Tune was scoring a number of tries on the other wing. He even scored one of them on my wing after I got caught up in the play. Fortune favours the brave, I suppose.

Mark McBain often advised me against getting frustrated about failing to get across the line. 'Don't worry about it,' he said. 'It's going to come.' The other players were good, too. Players like Ben Tune, Chris Latham, Toutai Kefu — they encouraged me a lot, telling me I just needed to get my hands on the ball more to make things happen. I was also aware of the fact that although I wasn't scoring tries, the opposition teams were paying me a lot of attention. This was a bad thing for me, because it meant I was attracting defence and therefore not getting the space I needed, but it was a good thing for my team-mates, because it meant I was creating openings for them.

When I still hadn't scored a try after six Super 12 matches, I began to wonder myself if I was somehow jinxed. Not all the statistics were bad. At this stage of the season I'd been breaking more tackles than any other Australian winger in the Super 12 competition. Someone who'd been keeping count worked out that I'd busted 4.1 tackles on average each match. But scoring tries is what really counts, and on this score I trailed other wingers badly. While I hadn't scored even one, Scott Staniforth had scored seven for the Waratahs, Graeme Bond had scored five for the Brumbies, and Marc Stcherbina, of the Waratahs, had scored four. One of the papers also pointed out that while I hadn't scored a try in my last five games for the Reds, I had scored seven in my last five games for the Broncos. Wally Lewis picked up on this. He was quoted in the *Sunday Telegraph* saying, 'They are not using Wendell as Wendell was used in rugby league, when the ball was thrown out to him on the wing and he was fairly destructive.'

Our seventh match was against the Bulls at Brisbane. The Bulls were one of the weaker teams in the competition. If any of us was going to score a try, it would probably be against them. Early in the match I almost did it. I made a half-break and was pulled down short of the line. After that there was a double-cut move. Steve Kefu went across the field and cut me under. Suddenly, I had the ball in my hands and I could see the line ahead of me. There was no way anyone would stop me now. I went over for the try and at that moment I had the greatest feeling of relief I've ever had in my life. The boys gathered around me. They knew how frustrated I'd been, and I think they were all genuinely happy for me. In fact, we were all so happy that we dropped our intensity for a few minutes and the let the Bulls in for a try.

> *That big hairy gorilla that has been sitting there on my back, it's gone. It started as a monkey, but it grew every week. I was getting a bit tired from carrying it around.*
>
> _____
>
> **WENDELL SAILOR**, DESCRIBING HIS RELIEF AT FINALLY SCORING A TRY IN SUPER 12.
> QUOTED BY DANNY WEIDLER IN THE *SUN-HERALD*.

I scored again in the second half. Elton Flatley made a half-break, about 35 metres out. I was on his inside and screaming for the ball. Sure enough, he gave it to me, and I ran in to score under the posts. So having played all those matches with the Reds without scoring a try, I'd now scored two in one match.

Why was that first try so long in coming? Are tries harder to score in union? My view is that in one way, yes, tries are harder to score in union, and the main reason for this is that in union there are two more defenders on the field. Playing for the Broncos, I always knew that once I broke the first line I'd just have to beat the fullback and I was away. Eight times out of 10 that would happen and I'd score. In union, when you break the first line, you still have a couple of big backrowers coming across at you. That's what I found hardest: you'd make a half-break but then have a couple of defenders come in. More people, more defence.

My other problem was simply that I was new to the code. Timing is everything when it comes to scoring tries. That's why Chris Latham scores so many: his timing is second to none. But timing in one code is different from timing in another, and timing only comes with experience. That is why I'm absolutely confident that I'll score a lot more tries for the Reds in 2003.

CAMPO AND ME

During my first full year in rugby, 2002, David Campese was probably my severest critic in the media. He said a number of times in his newspaper column that he didn't think I had what it took to make it in union. I had a shot back at him, but he kept bagging me, and eventually many people probably wondered if there was some type of a feud between us. There wasn't. I don't hold anything against Campese personally, and I certainly hope he doesn't hold anything against me. In fact, at one stage he seemed to be a big admirer of mine. That was when he wanted to become my manager.

After my previous manager, Barry Collins, and I ended our relationship, Campese's management company approached me, wanting to take over my affairs, and I was interested enough to have a game of golf with Campo's associate, Daryl McGraw. The first time I met Campo himself was after the Jack Newton golf tournament in 2000, when I gave him a lift back to his hotel. At that time people in the media were already speculating that I might switch from league, and as we drove back to Campo's hotel he told me he was confident I'd be a great success in union although he thought I'd have to improve one or two skills, such as kicking, and he offered to give me a hand in this regard if I needed it. But whether I switched or not, he told me his company could do a lot for me.

Campese's company was one of three or four at that time that were keen to sign me up. I considered its proposal carefully. After all, George Gregan was one of Campo's clients, and obviously George knew what he was doing. In the end, though, I decided to go with AMI, one of the main reasons being that it had offices in both Brisbane and Sydney as well as connections with New Zealand and Europe. It was run in Australia by Greg Keenan, a former league player and solicitor, and already had a few big names in union on his books — Stephen Larkham and Tana Umaga were two of them — a fact which impressed me. Out of courtesy, I phoned Daryl McGraw to tell him of my decision. He said that he was sorry and that he really felt Campese's company could have done a good job for me, and he said that if I changed my mind or if I ever needed a hand just to give him a call.

A few weeks after I signed with AMI, Campese said some negative things about me in his column in *The Australian*. To be honest, I didn't see the column myself: I was told about it by a journalist who phoned to get my reaction to it. According to the journalist, the gist of what Campese said was that I'd struggle to make it in union, that I wouldn't know how to run lines, that the backline moves would be different from anything I'd done in league, and so on.

When I heard all this I did my block. I didn't have a problem with Campese bagging me. As far as I was concerned, he was a legend in rugby, maybe the greatest player of his era, so he was entitled to speak his mind about anything in the game. What got up my nose was that he'd said exactly the opposite to me when he was wanting to sign me up as a client. I thought to myself, 'How on earth could he say one day that I'd make it in union and the next say that I'd struggle to make it?' I was so fired up I teed off on Campese to the journalist. I said something to the effect that while I knew that David Campese had the runs on the board, that he was a great player in his day, I'd be happy to play against him on the wing every day of the week because I'd use him as a doormat.

So next day the paper quoted me with headlines saying that I'd boasted I could use Campese as a doormat. I'd cooled down by then, and I wished I hadn't said as much as I had. Then, a few days later, I had a phone call from Daryl McGraw, who told me that Campo hadn't said the things about me that he was supposed to have said — that he had been taken out of context. I thanked McGraw for the call and admitted that I should have checked exactly what Campo had said before sounding off. After that, I got a call from Campo himself, more or less repeating what McGraw had said. I respected Campese for that and told him so.

The whole affair was one I wish hadn't happened. I felt I'd put my foot in my mouth. Campese was a bigger name in rugby than I could ever be, and regardless of what he had or hadn't said about me it was wrong of me to make the derogatory comment about him that I did. Someone who had achieved as much as he had in rugby didn't deserve that. Still, we ended this particular run-in all on good terms, and he offered again to give me advice or help if I needed it.

But Campo did not give up criticising me. At the end of the Super 12 season in 2002 he was quoted in the *Sydney Morning Herald* saying he thought my form overall had been very ordinary, and he had a shot at me in particular for not being able to get past the halfback, Chris Whitaker, in the match against the Waratahs. This was at a time when other former Wallabies were telling the media I had made a lot of progress and that my future looked bright.

There was worse to come. After I was picked to play my first Test against France in June 2000, Campese bagged me in his column. Here is what he said, 'The methods for selecting Test players must have changed if this Australian side is anything to go by. For example, Wendell Sailor was caught out of position time and time again last weekend against the Maori and yet he gets named. It just seems Wendell has been given a red-carpet ride to Test selection. To become a dual international is obviously a great achievement but when you look at previous dual inter-nationals, like Michael O'Connor, they were exceptional players who performed week in and week out. I cannot see Wendell in that mould. I'm still amazed to think there were players in Super 12 this year who performed consistently at a high standard — like Andrew Walker — and they're overlooked. Yes, Wendell's big. Yes, he's strong and, yes, he's getting paid a lot of money. So maybe we want to see some return on that investment. But does all that justify why he's been selected?'

I thought it was rough of Campese to suggest that I'd been picked because I was on a big contract and that rugby needed to get its money's worth — rough on me and rough on the selectors. Having made the mistake of reacting too quickly to Campese before, I made sure I kept quiet this time — at least to the media. Eddie Jones didn't keep quiet. He made a statement to the media saying he resented Campese suggesting that he and the other selectors had been pressured by the ARU to pick me, which he said was an attack on his integrity. Referring to Mat Rogers and me, he said, 'Both of them have got a fair way to go in some degree in their rugby education, but they've done enough to be in the best 23 at the moment.'

My former Bronco team-mate Lote Tuqiri had a shot at Campese, too. 'He's finished now, he's had his time in the sun,' he said. 'He should let Wendell get on with his career.' Lote also said, 'Wendell won't worry about what Campese says. He'll just prove him wrong like he has most of his critics over the years.' I heard that Campo gave Lote a bit of stick in the media, too, so maybe they came out even.

I might think Campo was wrong and unfair in his criticism of me, but I don't hold anything against him personally for saying what he said. What I do say is that he should be more constructive when he criticises. That's the difference with John Connolly. He often bagged me in his column, but he usually did it in a constructive way. Sometimes, being honest, I agreed with the criticisms that Connolly directed at me. Campo just fires his broadside, does his damage and that's it. Maybe he does it to be controversial. Or maybe it's because that's what the media wants.

No matter what he says about me, I will always be a big fan of Campo as a player. I often watched him in action when I was a young league player, and since then I've seen plenty of tapes of him when he was at his peak. Quite a few of us Broncos used to study what he did — it was another example of the mutual respect that has always existed between the two codes at the player level. We'd watch the rugby internationals and then we'd talk about the players among ourselves: 'That Campese — how good is he!'

I personally thought Campese's skills were unbelievable. Funnily enough, Chris Latham reminds me of Campo in some respects.

Like Campo, he is always looking to do something out of the ordinary — chipping and chasing, stepping through a clutch of defenders, flicking the unexpected pass and so on. Like Campo, he sometimes stuffs up, too, but more often than not he manages to pull it off and, every so often, like Campo, he does something that wins the match.

After I transferred to union I discovered that Campese and I had something in common apart from both being wingers: I like to sit at the front of the team bus and so did he. In both codes, the trendy thing is to sit at the back of the bus, but I've always liked to sit as close to the front window as possible, because you have a better view there and you get off the bus first. For years, I sat at the front of the Australian league team's bus. When I joined the Reds, the blokes at the back of the bus had a shot at me when I sat up the front. 'Hey, boys!' they called out. 'We've got another Campo.'

ROAD RAGE
AND THE WARATAHS

The 'road rage' incident that made so much news near the end of the Super 12 competition could not have come at a worse time for me — or so I thought when it happened. It was the day before our Super 12 match against the Waratahs. No matter what sport you're playing, a match between Queensland and NSW is super-important for everyone concerned. After I joined the Reds I soon found out (if I hadn't known it before) that the Waratahs' match was *the* big event of the year. From the moment we finished our match against the Sharks in South Africa, where Chris Latham got us out of jail, the only thing the boys could talk about was the match against the Waratahs the next weekend. They weren't tensed up about it. They just couldn't wait to get on the field. They had total belief in themselves.

This match at Ballymore was important for me personally. It was the last round but one of the Super 12 competition and, I thought, maybe my best chance to stake a claim for a Test spot. In fact, I had a strong feeling that any hope I had of making the Wallaby squad would depend on how I went in this match. I guessed all the Wallaby selectors would be there.

So the 'road rage' thing was a distraction at a time when I needed to be completely focused on my game. This is what happened. It was mid-morning on Saturday and I was on my way to golf. I was driving along the Western Freeway in Brisbane when a truck with two blokes in it cut me off. I was travelling at 90 to 100 km/h at the time, so I felt I could easily have had an accident. I caught up with the other vehicle and got the driver to pull over. I had a go at him, and he said, 'Sorry, mate, I didn't see you.' I felt I'd made my point and was turning to go back to my car when I heard one of them — it may have been the bloke on the passenger side — start laughing. I said to them, 'So you think it's funny, do you?' I was now really ropeable, and I thumped a window of the car with my hand and the glass broke.

As soon as I did it, I wished I hadn't. Tara wished I hadn't, too, when I arrived home with a cut hand and told her about it. I knew the story would get out and the media would go berserk over it, and I was filthy with myself for doing what I did. I should never have landed myself in a situation like this the day before a big game. Sure enough, the story broke big-time. The television news was full of it, and the headline in the paper next morning said, 'Sailor in road rage incident'. I publicly apologised to the other driver and I made a statement to the media expressing my regret at what had happened. I meant what I said.

So on the day of the match I had a lot on my mind apart from the match itself. There were three players in the Waratah team who were going for the same place that I was — Marc Stcherbina and Scott Staniforth, two wingers who were both playing well, and Matty Rogers, who was good enough to play just about anywhere in the backs. This is why matches between teams from the same country have an edge to them: everyone on the field is competing for positions in the same national team, so it all tends to get a bit personal. On top of that, there was the special tension that builds up before every match between Queensland and NSW, no matter what the sport. All season the other Reds had been saying to me, 'Wait until we play the Waratahs. We've got the wood on them and we've got to keep winning.'

> *I was yesterday involved in a traffic accident which I thought endangered my life. Unfortunately and regrettably, a window was broken in the incident. I smashed the window. The other two guys who were involved obviously thought it was a laughing matter. I thought it was a bit more personal than that, and I don't think I was in the wrong. I am very sorry it happened, and I regret that it did happen.*

WENDELL SAILOR, IN HIS STATEMENT TO THE MEDIA AFTER THE 'ROAD RAGE' INCIDENT, MAY 2002.

So, as I say, the 'road rage' thing couldn't have happened at a worse time. I was angry with myself because I knew the incident could cost me a place in the Test squad if it upset my focus and prevented me playing at my best against the Waratahs. Mark McBain must have noticed this when I phoned on the Saturday evening to explain to him personally what had happened. He later spoke about the mood I was in. 'Just talking to him,' he told the media, 'I knew he was fired up and raring to go.'

I definitely was raring to go, and I dearly wanted to score a try or two. This didn't happen, but I did have a good game. In fact, it was my best game of the whole Super 12 season, and even the NSW media said I'd done well. Greg Growden of the *Sydney Morning Herald* said, 'On an emotional weekend, Sailor was involved in a road rage incident in which a car window was smashed and was a prime instigator of the Queensland victory over NSW, setting up the match-winning try in the 48th minute.' He wrote that I'd gone 'on a wild, harum-scarum run around Ballymore that provided the break that led to a try by Reds' No.8, John Roe'. What I did was zip across the field beating five or six defenders, each time by stepping off my left foot. Roe scored in the next passage of play.

The Waratahs' coach, Bob Dwyer, thought I had a good game, too. He said that my 'harum-scarum' run was a turning point of the match. He also thought I deserved a place in the Wallaby squad. 'I've said for some weeks I think he's been going pretty well,' Dwyer said. 'He consistently beats the first tackle and today beat quite a few more. I don't think he's as good as he's going to be, but certainly if I was taking an extended squad into camp I would definitely take Mat Rogers and Wendell Sailor.' The one big let-down of the match for me was failing to score a try when I only had the halfback, Chris Whitaker, to beat. This was the play that earned me the bagging from David Campese that I referred to in the previous chapter. I have to admit that I did mess up, and I blame my ego for that. The ball came to me when I was about 20 metres from the line, and I could have scored easily if I'd gone for the corner. But I was cocky enough to believe that nobody —
certainly not someone of Chris Whitaker's size — could stop me

from that position, so I decided to take him on, to run through him instead of past him. In other words, I didn't give him the respect he deserved as a defender, which was a big mistake.

Whitaker pulled off a top tackle and brought me down a few metres from the line. As I hit the ground I remember thinking to myself, 'I can't believe I did that — I can't believe I let myself get tackled just short of the line.' Overconfidence had been my undoing. Good luck to Whitaker. It was a great play by him. The other Reds wouldn't let me live it down, though. Even in the Wallaby camp, some of the boys had a go at me, saying, 'Del, have you ever run under Whits before?' The funny thing was that towards the end of the Waratahs' game Junior Pelesasa scored, and he had to get past Whitaker to do it. Junior is about 10 kilograms lighter than me, but he was able to palm Whits off easily and go over in the corner. When I saw that happen and thought back to the try I'd just missed, I said to myself, 'It could only happen to me.'

[Sailor] was a prime instigator of the Queensland victory over NSW, setting up the match-winning try in the 48th minute. Sailor, who has been in fair-to-middling form since moving across from the Broncos and Kangaroos rugby league ranks this season, went on a harum-scarum ran around Ballymore that provided the break that led to a try by Reds' No.8, John Roe.

GREG GROWDEN, WRITING IN THE *SYDNEY MORNING HERALD*, MAY 2002.

Whether or not my 'harum-scarum' run was a turning point of the match, as Bob Dwyer suggested it was, my overall performance against the Waratahs was for me the turning point of the whole season. I'd enjoyed myself, I'd got involved, I'd done plenty of work, and I felt I'd more than held my own against my opposite number, Scott Staniforth. All in all, I had a good game — my best game of the Super 12 season, in fact — but it would have been better still if I'd got through the Whitaker tackle. I never feel really satisfied with how I perform in a game unless I score a try, and I definitely should have scored then. But that was the only let-down. The crowd was big — and excited — which made it all the more memorable an occasion. In fact, I'd say the Ballymore crowd that day was one of the best I've played in front of.

But the 'road rage' incident hadn't gone away. Jeff Miller suggested I should make a public apology for what had happened, and I was happy to do that. So after the match I gave a media conference. Usually, only three or four reporters turn up for a post-match conference, but this day there must have been at least 15 of them — from newspapers, radio, television, the lot. This in itself made me realise how a fairly minor incident had grown into something big. As I was walking out of the room at the end of the media conference, one of the reporters said to me, 'Wendell, do you think you need anger management?' The question irritated me and I felt like reacting, but I let it go and kept walking — just as I should have let what happened on the Western Freeway go.

Mark McBain also seemed confident about my chances of making the Wallaby squad. He was asked afterwards if I was ready to play for the Wallabies. He replied, 'Yes … simple as that. You wouldn't put him on the bench.'

A WALLABY AT LAST

By the end of the Super 12 season in 2002 a lot of people seemed to think that because I hadn't scored as many tries for the Reds as I had for the Broncos I must be feeling disappointed with myself. The opposite was true. I felt very satisfied with how I'd performed. I'd accomplished more than, realistically, I'd thought I could. It was true that I'd scored only a couple of tries in Super 12, but I honestly believed I'd played pretty soundly overall and hadn't made many mistakes. I certainly hadn't let the Queensland team down, which had been my greatest fear. Most important of all, I felt I'd at last settled into rugby. I hadn't mastered the game, of course, but I'd certainly got the hang of it. I no longer felt like a novice.

Not long after the Super 12 season was over, I was pleased to see Andrew Slack quoted in a Sydney paper saying that he thought I'd done well. Andrew had just been chosen to take over from Mark McBain as the Reds' coach for 2002, and he was apparently asked what he thought of me. He said, 'Anything that Wendell's done will only be improved upon, and I think what he has done is damn good. If Wendell had come from 20 years of playing rugby, people would say he'd had a damn solid season — made a few blues, but who hasn't? But because he's been under such intense scrutiny, those who were critical of him coming over can't see the good things.'

A damn solid season! That's as much as I'd hoped for in my first year in rugby. I just wanted to establish myself in the game at the Super 12 level so I'd be in a position to make a big push for a place in the Wallabies in 2003. I thought I might make a squad of 28 for an end-of-year tour of Europe as the third or fourth winger, but I never gave myself a realistic chance of being picked to play in a Test in 2002 unless something really unexpected happened.

Something unexpected did happen. Our last Super 12 match was against the Otago Highlanders on 11 May, and after that we all went back to play club rugby — in my case, for the Gold Coast Breakers. In the meantime, Eddie Jones had phoned to say that I'd been picked to play for Australia A against Canada on 1 June. He also told me I'd be on the right wing, which, as a left-foot stepper, has always been my preferred side. In fact, I've been a left-foot stepper since I was seven or eight years old. Recently I watched some tapes of myself playing as a schoolboy, and I noticed that I nearly always stepped off my left foot even then.

Not long before that Australia A game, word came through that Ben Tune had done his knee in a club match. I heard the news with mixed feelings. Ben's a really nice guy and he'd been very good to me ever since I switched to union, always willing to help me out with advice, and I naturally wished the best for him. At the same time, I could see that his injury might open a door for me.

I phoned him to see how he was. I was a bit surprised to find him in good spirits — this may have been because he'd had so many injuries over the years that he'd learned to take them in his stride. He told me he'd probably be out for four to six weeks, and he encouraged me to make the most of his absence, which was pretty generous of him. He wished me all the best in the Australia A game the following week and said he hoped that, as a fellow Queenslander, I could fill his position.

So all of a sudden there was a vacancy to fill, and I was in the running to fill it. This had come from Eddie Jones himself. He had been quoted tipping Mat Rogers and me to play for Australia A against Canada. 'Both have had very positive Super 12s', he said, 'and guys who've done well in the Super 12 have every chance of being selected in Australia A.' Reading this gave me a lift because, to be honest, I wasn't sure I'd done enough in Super 12 to be first replacement as a winger for the Wallabies. After all, there were other wingers with very good credentials, Andrew Walker being one.

The Australia A game was obviously meant to be a trial for the internationals to follow. When we went into camp before it Eddie Jones said to me, 'Mate, there's a big opportunity for you here. There are positions up for grabs, and if you play well against Canada you'll be right in the running.' By now I'd begun training with players who'd been opponents in the Super 12 — people like Graeme Bond, a player I'd respected all year, David Lyons and, of course, Mat Rogers.

The game against Canada was played at Parramatta Stadium, which was familiar territory for me. Knowing that a place in the Test side was up for grabs, I was determined to produce a big performance. As things turned out, we beat the Canadians 102–8, so the match did not prove a lot, but I did score two tries and made a few other good runs. Mat Rogers scored three tries, and each of us set up a try for the other. Next morning I was interested to read Danny Weidler saying in the *Sun-Herald* that I was a sure thing for Test selection. He wrote, 'With Ben Tune out injured,

Sailor went into yesterday's game only needing a solid performance to guarantee a spot on the right wing — and he impressed
those who matter with a damaging two-try display.'

Weidler was more confident than I was, but he turned out to
be right. I was picked in the Wallaby team to play New Zealand
Maori in Perth on 15 June. The game wasn't a Test, of course, but
it was an official Australian team that played in it, so this was my
debut as a Wallaby. Plenty of my league mates phoned to wish me
luck — Andrew Johns, Darren Lockyer, Lote Tuqiri, Alfie Langer.
They called to say that they'd be watching and that they hoped
I'd have a great game. Wayne Bennett phoned me, too. He told me
to go out and play the game and not try to do anything special.

*I've said for some weeks that I think he's been going pretty well.
He consistently beats the first tackle and today beat quite a few
more. I don't think he's as good as he's going to be, but certainly,
if I was taking an extended squad into camp, I would definitely
take Mat Rogers and Wendell Sailor.*

BOB DWYER, COMMENTING ON SAILOR'S FORM
AFTER THE REDS-WARATAHS SUPER 12 MATCH, MAY 2002.
QUOTED BY STEVE CONNOLLY OF AAP.

Before I knew it, there I was in a Wallaby jersey, warming up
with players like George Gregan, Stephen Larkham and Matt
Burke. The anthem was sung, the Maori players did their haka

and, suddenly, play was under way. Just over two minutes into the match there was a ruck not far from the Maori line. I came off the right wing, took a short pass from Daniel Herbert and made a dash for the line. I broke through one tackle and thought I was in the clear, but somehow one of the Maori backs, Ryan Nicholas, managed to ankle-tap me and bring me down. I saw the way to the line was still open, so I got to my feet, took off again and touched down for a try without anyone putting another hand on me. I was so focused during those last few strides to the line that I felt I was moving in slow motion. As I dived over the line one of the Maori players hit me with a cheap shot, which gave me a massive lump on my head, but I was so numb with the excitement of the moment that I don't think I felt it.

My career as a Wallaby couldn't have had a better start than this. It had taken me eight weeks to score a try in Super 12, and now I'd scored one 2 minutes and 49 seconds into my first appearance as a Wallaby. I was a bit dazed from the blow to the head, but I was still able to enjoy the congratulations I got from the other Wallabies, George Gregan included. It felt so good to be running on the right wing again, my old position. I felt so much more at ease.

In the end, it was just as well I scored that try. After trailing 6–20 at one stage, the Maori came back strongly in the second half, throwing the ball around, and in one passage of play they had 14 or 15 phases in a row. Their comeback was engineered by Carlos Spencer, a player I have tremendous respect for. In fact, I put him in the Darren Lockyer class. I was praying that we'd hold out for a win — apart from anything else, I didn't want my try to have been in vain — and we just managed to do that. The final score was 27–23.

He took a short pass from Daniel Herbert and smashed through the tackle of Mark Mayerhofler (a noted defender), rolled and then plunged across the line for a try. Momentum is an equation that combines speed and weight. Jonah Lomu and Sailor have both. The power this momentum generates works best at the Test match level of rugby. At other levels, teams can detail several players to mark the Big Man. Do this in Tests and gaps are left for the other players to run through. So Sailor, with his ability to make direct breaks, is assured of a place in the Wallaby squad.

SPIRO ZAVOS, SYDNEY MORNING HERALD RUGBY COLUMNIST, COMMENTING ON SAILOR'S DEBUT AS A WALLABY AGAINST THE NEW ZEALAND MAORI, JUNE 2002.

Apart from scoring the try, I felt I'd had a good game. I did get criticised for my positional play, especially in defence. Spiro Zavos, a Sydney rugby columnist, suggested I was to blame for letting in one or two tries. He said, 'Twice Sailor was caught in no-man's land with several runners coming at him. Instead of holding his position, he came in to tackle the runner and the gap was created.' I do admit to doing this once. It was an error of judgment. Two runners were coming at me and I went to put a big shot on one of them, but he threw a pass over my head and a Maori player scored in the corner. At the end of the game I was speaking to George Gregan and Toutai Kefu. I told them how bad I felt about coming off my line, but they said not to worry, that I was being tough on myself. It was a costly mistake for the Wallabies, and I had learned a lesson the hard way.

> *One of the highlights for me was playing and training in the same side as Wendell Sailor. In a camp situation he is great value. Not all the boys knew each other, but Wendell would start into someone and all of a sudden everyone would be having a go and their personalities would emerge.*
>
> **MAT ROGERS**, WRITING IN THE *SUN-HERALD* AFTER HE AND SAILOR PLAYED FOR AUSTRALIA A AGAINST CANADA, JUNE 2002.

Despite this error, Zavos thought I'd make the Wallaby team because I showed I could break tackles and get through a defensive line. Others agreed with him. In fact, in Monday's papers I was generally tipped to make the starting line-up again in the Test against France at the Colonial Stadium in Melbourne on the following Saturday. This was what I wanted to hear, because I knew that my chances of making the Test side against France depended on how well I'd played against the Maori. By now, Scott Staniforth had injured his shoulder and was out of contention, but there were other wingers pushing for a place in the side. If I hadn't played well against the Maori, Andrew Walker would probably have got the nod for the right wing spot. Or maybe Mat Rogers. The big question was whether Eddie Jones thought I'd had a good game against the Maori. His opinion was the one that really counted.

During this time I'd gradually begun to settle into the Wallaby camp and feel part of the group. The Wallabies are a very tight unit, but I was made to feel accepted. Naturally, it took me a while to get to know all the other players. Stephen Larkham is an example. I don't think I spoke to him more than two or three times during the first month I spent in the Wallaby camp. He seemed so quiet. Then I got to know him better and discovered that he is actually quite a funny guy, with a personality all his own.

I can honestly say that not one of the Wallabies ever said or did anything to make me feel, as a recruit from league, that I was unwelcome. I think Matty Rogers would say the same. Sure, they did have a go at me from time to time. Later, when I'd been dropped from the Wallaby team but was still in the squad, we were sitting around one day and I piped up with, 'Boys, I'm just a club rugby player now.' They all howled at me, saying, 'Club rugby player! Mate, you're on half a million dollars.' One of the regular Wallabies said, 'Del, how can you be just a club rugby player when you're earning twice as much as I am?' I came back saying that all these big-money sums were just newspaper talk and that it surprised me that people with their experience would believe everything they read in the papers. So we all had a bit of fun with it, but there was never any malice.

THE PINNACLE

The match against the Maori was played on 15 June. The first Test against France was to be played one week later, on 22 June. There were quite a few of us who seemed a chance to make the team, but no more than that, and I think we were all on tenterhooks for the first day or two of that week. What was Eddie Jones thinking, we all wondered? To begin with, Eddie gave nothing away. I had a meeting with him early in the week, and he said something to the effect that he was pleased with my progress. But that was all. He didn't give any hint as to whether I'd make the Test side that Saturday. Then, on Wednesday, we had another one-on-one meeting. After chatting for a while he told me he liked the way I played against the Maori. Then he said, 'This week you'll be on the right wing against France.'

I'd played for some top teams in my time, the State of Origin and Australian league sides among them, but I'd never felt so pumped at being selected as I did when Eddie Jones told me I'd made the Wallaby Test side. This was what I'd been aiming for ever since I first thought of switching to union. This was the pinnacle. I have no idea what I said in reply to Eddie. All I remember is thinking to myself, 'How good is this — I'm going to be a dual international after all!'

As soon as the meeting with Eddie was over I got on the phone. First I called Tara to tell her the news. Then my mother. Then a few of my mates — blokes like Lote Tuqiri, Darren Lockyer, Gorden Tallis. Mum was thrilled, not just for my sake but, I think, for Dad's sake, too. I asked her if I could fly her down to Melbourne for the match, but she said no, she'd just watch it on television. My mother had come down to a couple of Super 12 matches in Brisbane, but that's as far as she wanted to travel from Sarina. Flying to Perth (I wanted her to come over and see me play against the Maori) or even Melbourne was too much. If I get to play in the World Cup in 2003 I'll be trying hard to get her to come and see one or two of the matches, but if they're not played in Queensland it won't be easy.

The key interest for Australians was in Wendell Sailor, making his debut for the Wallabies out on the wing. The good news was that every time he touched the ball, voltage moved through the crowd. Like David Campese at his best, Sailor has the capacity to generate enormous surges of excitement with just the thought of what he might do. When he does it, it is a bonus.

PETER FITZSIMONS, COMMENTING IN THE *SYDNEY MORNING HERALD* ON SAILOR'S RUGBY TEST DEBUT AGAINST FRANCE.

So I had a lot to celebrate, but in the middle of it all I found myself missing my father a lot. Ever since I was a boy, Dad had been part of my successes in sport. In fact, one of the best things for me about doing well in sport, especially rugby league, was seeing how happy it made my father. Making Dad proud of me was always one of my motivations as a footballer. Now he was gone, and while I couldn't have been more stoked at making the Test side, I really missed being able to share the moment with him — this was the first time in my nine years as a professional footballer that Dad had not been there to enjoy my success.

For me, the only other sour note of that week was David Campese's attack on me in his newspaper column. As recounted in an earlier chapter, Campese wrote that I didn't deserve to be in the team, and he hinted that the selectors had picked me because the ARU was paying me a lot and needed a return on its investment. Campo's article caused a bit of a stir inside the Australian camp, and Eddie Jones was asked if he thought I'd be thrown off balance by the whole controversy. He replied, 'I think Wendell's more worried whether people think his earrings are diamonds or not.'

It was good of Eddie to say this, but it wasn't entirely true. Campo's article did throw me off balance. After it appeared, I spoke to some of the other Wallabies about it. They said not to let it bother me — that Campo was just sounding off and that no-body would take too much notice. But it did bother me. I wouldn't have been human if it didn't. After all, what he said was pretty damaging. I can't remember the same thing being said about any other footballer, league or union — that is, that I may have made the team for commercial reasons, not because I was a good enough player. I tried to close my mind to it, but the whole issue definitely put extra pressure on me in the days leading up to the Test.

Maybe it affected the way I played on the day. What I focused on that day in Melbourne was not making a mistake. I was conscious of the fact that my position in the team was under question, so I tried to play safe. I did this successfully. I didn't make a single mistake that I can remember. I didn't miss a tackle. I didn't drop a ball. On the other hand, I didn't make a big impact on the game in a positive way either. I made a few half-breaks, but that was about it. What surprised me was that the French did not do what everyone was tipping them to do: namely, turn me around by kicking the ball behind me — a tactic teams have often used against Jonah Lomu. I was waiting for it, but it didn't happen. In a way, I was disappointed about this, because I was keen to run the ball back at them.

Opinions in the media on my debut were mixed. This is what Peter FitzSimons wrote in Monday's *Sydney Morning Herald*: 'With Sailor's first touch he was able, as advertised, to break three tackles, swerve past another two and surge the play 30 metres downfield. Against that, in the first 10 minutes of the game, when the French fullback hit the line and charged down Sailor's side of the field, the league convert was nowhere to be seen. At least not in that vicinity. He was on the far side of the field, trotting back, rather as one does in rugby league after making a good tackle.' FitzSimons went on to say that he spoke to two Australian coaches after the match, Bob Dwyer and Rod Macqueen, and suggested to them that I'd been out of position. They didn't agree. They thought I'd had a good game, done a lot of work and so on.

My own opinion was that I hadn't messed up but that I could have done more. I felt disappointed that I hadn't made a bigger contribution to Australia's win. Eddie Jones felt the same way.

He spoke to me about it the following week. By this time, I'd had my position in the team confirmed for the second Test against France on 29 June, one week after the first Test. Eddie said, 'Your debut was sound and you didn't make a mistake, but you were playing cautiously.' I said, 'That's true. I knew a lot of people would be watching, I had Campo's comment at the back of my head and I just didn't want to stuff up on my debut.' Eddie said, 'Okay. But next week I want you to get out there and make the most of it. I want you to take them on.'

The second Test was played at Stadium Australia in Sydney before a big crowd. My performance was the opposite of my performance in the first Test, because I set out to play more adventurously. In the first Test I didn't make a mistake. Here, I made several. I missed a couple of tackles I wouldn't normally miss, and I dropped a ball in full view of everyone. Matty Rogers gave me the ball about 15 metres from the French line. There was a hole for me to go through, and I think I was looking at the hole instead of the ball when I dropped the pass. On the other hand, I made a few good runs and I did help set up a try. Australia won again, so after three matches with the Wallabies I hadn't yet been on the losing side.

Playing against the French rugby union team was a new experience for me, of course, and I was impressed by them. They played tough, they were very aggressive, and they were great athletes. I would like to have got to know a few of their players, but there wasn't time for that.

My performance in the second Test was a mixed bag, but it was obviously not good enough to keep me in the starting line-up after Ben Tune became available again, which he did in time for the first Tri-Nations match against New Zealand in Christchurch.

There was no way I'd displace Ben. As I see it, he's currently the best winger in both rugby codes in Australia. In fact, the only winger who would compare with him anywhere, in my opinion, is Jason Robinson of England, a player I've always had tremendous respect for. There didn't seem any chance, either, that they'd drop Stirling Mortlock, because he'd been playing really well all season.

I did have some hope, though, that I'd keep a place in the 22. Obviously, wingers don't normally get a seat on the bench, but I thought there was at least a chance that I'd be picked as an impact player who could come on in the second half and, if all went well, break the line. This has been Jonah Lomu's role in the All Blacks, and it was the role I was aiming for.

But it wasn't to be. Eddie Jones made it as easy for me as he could. He told me Ben would go back on the right wing and that there wouldn't be a place for me on the bench. I said I could understand that. I still had hopes of being picked for the bench and coming on as a game-breaker when we played the South Africans in Brisbane, though. I spoke to Eddie Jones about it, asking whether my only hope of getting into the team now was to make the starting XV. He confirmed this by saying that for the time being the bench was carrying an extra forward, and that each of the backs on the bench was indispensable.

This is how it is with the Wallabies: they're such consistent players that it's very rare for any of them to have a really bad game and get dropped, which makes it hard for an outsider to break in. Eddie did say that things might be different on the European tour at the end of the year — that I might have a place in the 22. 'You might get an opportunity there', he said, 'and if you do, you have to take it with both hands.'

In each of the Tri-Nations Tests there was a chance I'd come into the side to replace an injured player. Stirling Mortlock, Matt Burke and Mat Rogers were all 'under an injury cloud' at one time or another, and for a while Ben Tune looked in danger of being sidelined from the Test in South Africa over the so-called drugs affair. In fact, Eddie Jones let me know in advance that if Ben couldn't play I would go into the XV on the right wing, and I ran on the right wing at three training sessions in South Africa in Ben's absence. If a place had become vacant in any of these matches I would have been desperate to fill it, but in the end each of the players pulled through, so the opportunity didn't arise. Their good luck, my bad luck.

So I played club rugby with the Gold Coast Breakers and really enjoyed the three games I played. Unfortunately, we missed out on making the finals. As I remarked one day to Jeff Miller, this was the first time in my professional career that I'd ever been in a club team that hadn't made the finals.

Our last game was against Sunnybank. When we went off at half-time, the score was 12–all. I hadn't seen much ball that day and was feeling a bit frustrated. During the break, one of the other Breakers said to me, 'Del, do you realise you're one of only two out of 31 players in our team who haven't scored a try all season?' After my long tryless run with the Reds, that was the last thing I wanted to hear. I went back on the field determined to score, even if it meant hogging the ball. Not long into the second half the opposition centre, Jason Ramsamy, who was in the Reds squad with me, went to catch the ball and dropped it. I toed it ahead a few times. The last time I toed it I was afraid I'd kicked it too hard, and I prayed, 'Please don't let it go over the dead-ball line.' But it stopped just inside the in-goal and I scored. There were probably under 1000 people there, but when they cheered I felt so relieved. I was also excited, because I still get just as big a buzz from scoring a try in a club game as in an international. I scored again in that half, which meant I ended up with a respectable strike rate of two tries in three matches for the Breakers.

Eddie Jones did say to me that he thought I'd played well for the Wallabies and that I was ahead of where I'd been expected to be at this point. This was what I thought, too. In fact, when I achieved my ambition of becoming a dual international in the first French Test I felt I was about a year ahead of schedule.

POST-MORTEM

Although my first year in rugby union had its highs and lows, the important thing for me was that it did finish on a high. In fact, the last game I played in 2002 — the Test against Italy at Genoa on 23 November — was my best game of the whole year, and the second-last game I played, against England at Twickenham, was probably my second-best. This showed that my campaign to make it in union was still on track, that I was still improving as a player, and it gave me the lift I needed to go into 2003 full of confidence. I was so pumped up at the end of the European tour that I felt I couldn't wait for the World Cup year to begin.

I played in all four Tests on tour, the previous two being against Argentina and Ireland. The Ireland match was disappointing both for the team and for me. We lost — and I touched the ball only four times that I can remember. As one of the other Wallabies said to me later, 'It was a bad day for winger'. That happens in rugby. I kept searching for the ball, but the ball wasn't there. Unfortunately, I turned the ball over at my first touch. I ran into an Irish defender and had it jolted out of my hands. I didn't feel too badly about that, because it was a pretty solid collision. In fact, the other bloke was half-knocked out and had to go off at half-time. Otherwise, I didn't put a foot wrong.

We felt terrible about our loss to England, after leading by so much in the second half, but it was still a memorable experience for me, playing in front of 75,000 at Twickenham. I had a good game as well, even if one or two journos without much knowledge of the game thought otherwise. Eddie Jones was pleased with how I performed. 'Wendell,' he said, 'that's the level I want you playing to every week.' Even a few English players — Jason Robinson and Jonny Wilkinson were two of them — said to me afterwards that I'd had a good game.

One or two things did go wrong for me. At one point Elton Flatley turned the ball inside to me, but the pass went behind me and I slipped over. Otherwise, I thought I had a match that was just about mistake-free. My handling was good and I didn't miss a tackle. In fact, two tries may have been saved by tackles I made. Considering how much criticism there was of my defence earlier in the year, I was pleased that in four Tests on tour I didn't miss a single tackle. Not one. I felt that set the record straight.

The game statistics showed how involved I was in that England match. I did 10 tackles, not bad for a winger. I had 11 runs and did 10 clean-outs: more than 30 involvements in all. And, of course, I scored a try — my first in a Test. Stephen Larkham glided through a hole in the English defence and I was there to take the ball. It may not have been one of my better tries, but because I scored it against the old enemy, England, before a capacity crowd at Twickenham, it got my adrenalin pumping more than any try I'd ever scored.

Then came Italy. Without doubt, this was my best match as a union player so far — and I say that after making allowance for the fact that Italy wasn't the strongest side. I think the main reason

I was so on top of my game this day was that my performance against England the week before had lifted my confidence. I felt that if I could play well against England before a huge, partisan crowd on their home ground I could play well anywhere. So although the conditions for the Italy Test were terrible — wet and slippery — I went on feeling positive and ran the ball with as much confidence as I did for the Broncos.

> *You could have put him in a Brisbane Broncos jumper there tonight. That's what we have signed him for — to be the bloke in a one-on-one opportunity who can beat the guy, has power and you can use him in a variety of field positions. Wendell has just lacked confidence.*
>
> **EDDIE JONES**, WALLABY COACH, SPEAKING AFTER THE TEST AGAINST ITALY, NOVEMBER 2002.

This is what Greg Growden wrote in the *Sydney Morning Herald*: 'At last his [Sailor's] backline team-mates gave him some proper ball and space to work in, enabling him to make several bustling midfield runs in each half, the most impressive a 40-metre charge in the 32nd minute and a 50-metre gallop in the final quarter, which had Italian defenders sprawling.'

As I've mentioned elsewhere, I've had a niggling knee injury for some time which in 2002 became an increasing problem. It caused me so much trouble on the European tour that within two weeks of returning to Brisbane, in early December 2002, I went into hospital to have it operated on. All went well, and I'm confident the knee won't be a problem in 2003. One reason I'm confident is that my personal trainer, Mark Burgess, took charge of my rehabilitation. As well as being one of the best personal trainers in Brisbane, Mark is a mate of mine. He's also a motivator. He has such a positive outlook that I get a charge just from being in his company. During one period in 2002, when I was getting bagged on all sides, he sent me a text message on my mobile, saying, 'Remember this mate: tough times don't last, tough people do.' That struck a chord with me at the time.

So my first year as a union player was over. How did I go? On the face of it, I did well. I played a full Super 12 season with the Reds and I played for the Wallabies in six Tests, so becoming a dual international. If I'd been told at the start of the year that I'd do all this in 2002, I wouldn't have believed it. And yet, once the year was over, I felt frustrated as well as pleased, because I knew how much better I could have performed. If I had to put a figure on it, I would say that for much of 2002 I played to about 60 per cent of my ability. No more than that.

Why only 60 per cent? It wasn't that I'd somehow lost any of the ability I had at the Broncos to break the line and score tries — I'm sure of that. It wasn't that I'd suddenly got too old. What's the difference between 26 and 27, after all? And it wasn't that I wasn't as good physically as I was at the Broncos. I'll admit that I'd put on extra muscle and extra weight and lost a bit of speed, but in the overall picture these changes did not really count for much. I was basically the same footballer, physically, that I'd always been.

> *[Sailor] needs to get moving. I've noticed sometimes that he steps sideways without going forward. That's a problem players have when they come back from playing sevens football. He needs to get a video of Jonah Lomu and realise that the sideline is his friend. Lomu's great strength is getting the ball in his left hand and palming off with his right as he charges along. Because Sailor continually refuses to go to the sideline, defenders can swarm on him from either side, making him an easy target. I know Australian teams try to get Lomu to run in-field and Sailor is doing too much of that.*

JOHN CONNOLLY, WRITING IN THE *SUN-HERALD*, APRIL 2002.

Also, it wasn't that I'd run up against better defenders in union than I'd ever had to deal with in league, defenders who were able to stop me where league defenders couldn't. Union players may have improved their defence to a point where they tackle just as well now as league players, but they don't tackle any better. Sure, there are two more defenders in union than in league, and this did make it harder for me, but this still wouldn't explain why I played at only 60 per cent of my ability.

No, the main factor affecting my play in 2002 was the obvious one: I was new to the game. Apart from all the practical disadvantages of not knowing automatically what to do at any one moment, this affected the way I played in two major ways. One, it meant I wasn't able to do things instinctively as I'd always done in league. I had to think before I did anything, and I'm the type of footballer who always performs better when I follow my instincts and play without thinking. This undermined my game generally.

The other major way it affected my play was to eat into my confidence. I'm a confidence player — confidence has always been the key to my success in football — and I definitely wasn't the confident player on the rugby union field in 2002 that I had always been with the Broncos. I was still feeling my way and concentrating on not making mistakes.

Admitting all this may sound negative, but it's not. The problems I had in 2002 were probably inevitable: they were the problems anyone would face if he switched to another code of football with hardly any experience of how to play it. Also, they're only temporary problems, and I feel they are already behind me. I've now settled into rugby. The game isn't foreign to me any more. I've got over the problem of having to think, every moment of the game, where I ought to be and what I ought to be doing. Because of this, I know my confidence has come back. I can't wait for the 2003 season to start. I'll be running onto the field with a completely different attitude from the attitude I had in 2002. I'm totally confident that I'll be making as big an impact on the field in 2003 as I did with the Broncos.

I'm certainly determined that there won't be another long wait for a try in Super 12. I wouldn't have admitted it at the time, but going for seven rounds without a try in 2002 did get to me. Scoring tries had been second nature to me for so long that I couldn't work out how I was missing out. I used to watch the tapes of each match and wonder how it was that I hadn't gone on to score from this break or that half-break. If this had been a league match and I'd been playing for the Broncos, I knew for certain that I would have scored from there. The confidence and ego I had on the league field would have guaranteed that. So it became a big worry for me and was on my mind all the time. I'd go to training with the Reds feeling frustrated and depressed. Some of the boys could tell how I was feeling, and I remember Sam Cordingley, who was one of my mates in the team, doing his best to lift my spirits. 'You're playing good,' Sam said. 'You're making breaks. You're setting up plays. You're attracting defence. What are you worrying about?'

I was worrying because I wasn't scoring tries. For me, scoring tries wasn't just the icing on the cake — it was just about the whole cake! It was the reason I was on the field. I'm not the only one who feels like this. Blokes like Chris Walker, Steve Renouf and Lote Tuqiri are the same: they really love scoring tries. My frustration built up. I was stuck in a rut without a try and didn't know how to get out of it. I began to second-guess myself. I'd think, 'Have I lost it a bit or what? Am I too big, or too slow, or too old, or what?' The questions and the doubts swirled around in my head. I'd come home and say to Tara, 'What's going on? I'm working hard, I'm doing everything right, but I just can't cross that line.'

Looking back on it now, I think there were several reasons why I took so long to score a Super 12 try — poor positional play, poor timing on my part and, also, a fair bit of bad luck. I believe there was one other factor also working against me. The fact that you're having a bad run at anything always puts you under extra pressure, and then, because you're under pressure, the bad run is harder to break. In other words, it's self-perpetuating. One day I'd like to swap notes on this with Greg Chappell, because I suspect he struck the same problem all those years ago when he made a string of ducks.

I've talked here about the broad problems I had to deal with when I started playing rugby. There were also dozens of points of union technique that I had to adjust to, and not all of these could be learned from a book. Some I only picked up on as the season went along.

Here is one example. I said before that wing is the easiest position in union for a league player to learn. That's true, but even on the wing there are differences between the codes that aren't obvious at first but that you need to become aware of. Take the criticism of me by former Reds' coach John 'Knuckles' Connolly for not using the sideline enough. Now Connolly probably criticised me more often than anyone else in the media — more often even than Campo. He made it pretty clear, time after time, that he didn't think I had the know-how to play rugby union at the Test level. But not all his criticism was negative; sometimes he gave positive advice, and this was an example. He suggested that I should copy Jonah Lomu and try to crash through down the sideline, holding the ball in one hand and palming off defenders with the other. According to Connolly, running down the sideline meant Lomu had defenders coming at him from one side only, whereas because I kept clear of the sideline, I had defenders swarming on me from both sides.

Nobody likes agreeing with people who criticise them, but in this case I had to agree with Knuckles. Wayne Bennett would agree with him, too. If Wayne ever had a problem with the way I played on the wing for the Broncos, it was that I didn't back myself enough on the sideline, that I kept running in-field. Now that's not such a bad fault in league, because in league, about the worst thing a winger can do is lose possession by letting himself get forced into touch. Realising this, I developed a habit of coming back inside, and Wayne used to criticise me for it, saying that I had to take the sideline more. In union, being forced into touch isn't such a serious offence, because your team has a chance of regaining possession in the line-out, but it's hard to teach an old dog new tricks, and after I switched to union I still kept running inside. I'd been doing it for 10 years, so it was a hard habit to break. Eddie Jones picked me up on it, too, saying I had to make more use of the sideline.

So Knuckles was spot-on with what he said. It's true that the good wingers in union, guys like Jonah Lomu and Ben Tune, use the line. It's something I'm now very conscious of, and I'll be making sure that I use the line a lot more in 2003.

'With any player who has that much ability, you've got to give him the ball as much as possible. He has to just work out how he can be involved as much as possible. The more he touches the ball, the harder it is going to be for other teams ... [He is] the best winger I've played against. He is a very powerful guy and it takes a few people to stop him.'

JASON ROBINSON, ENGLISH CONVERT FROM LEAGUE TO UNION, SPEAKING ABOUT SAILOR BEFORE THE ENGLAND-AUSTRALIA MATCH IN NOVEMBER 2002, QUOTED BY GREG GROWDEN IN THE *SYDNEY MORNING HERALD*.

For me, the big plus of my first year in rugby — apart from the honour of becoming a dual international — was that I got through the learning process intact. I proved to myself that I can both break the line in union and draw defence, as I used to do in league. As I said before, I believe that drawing defence was one of my most valuable contributions to the Reds. I do a lot of homework on my performance after each match, watching passages of play over and over on tape, and I saw that time after time I attracted extra defence, which I'm sure is because of the type of power game that I play. It was particularly obvious when I came off my wing to take the ball from the five-eighth, Elton Flatley, and try to hit it up. Then I'd get swarmed on, because they obviously saw me as a danger. This can be frustrating for me, because I'm happiest when I have a bit of space to move in, but it's something a player of my type has to put up with.

Another big plus was being part of the Wallabies. I really mean this. The Wallabies are a very close bunch, like the Broncos, and it's always a good feeling to be part of a group as close as that. The fact that the Wallabies are so close is, I'm sure, one of the reasons they've been so successful. It's not just the players who are close. It's also the medical staff, the coaches, everyone connected with the team. I thought Glenn Ella was terrific as assistant coach. Glenn is really switched-on when it comes to rugby. He knows backline play inside out. He worked hard with me in the Sevens and later on in the Wallabies. If I ever wanted to get an opinion about some play I'd been involved in, he was always willing to pull out a tape and study it with me. He was positive right from the start. In fact, I remember him saying not long after I switched to union that the best thing the Reds could do was put me in the starting line-up straight away.

TARA

When I went across to rugby union, I didn't go alone: Tara and Tristan came with me. She was a rugby union recruit, too. This was one of the main reasons why the decision whether or not to switch codes wasn't one that I could take lightly. Going to union didn't mean an upheaval just for me; it would be an upheaval for Tara, too, which was something I had to think about. Tara was as much a part of the Broncos family as I was. The Broncos were the centre of our social life. Tara's friends were the wives and girlfriends of other Broncos, and she mixed with them all the time and took Tristan to their playgroup. If I went over to union, the odds were she'd find herself cut off from all this.

So switching to union was going to be a gamble for Tara as well as for me, so obviously there was no way I would have gone ahead with it if Tara wasn't 100 per cent behind the move. I talked to her about it from the time that the idea of switching first entered my head. Right from the start, she was very positive. She told me later that this was because she already had a feeling that I'd gone about as far in league as I could go. She sensed that I was getting restless, that I'd reached a point in my career where I needed a new challenge.

Tara's support was the green light for me to take the idea further. She maintained that support right through: from those first few weeks when going to union was just a crazy idea that we talked about to the moment when we finally decided to do it. Like me, Tara was entering a strange, new world when we went across to union. In fact, she'd had even less to do with union than me. Tara came from a league-mad family. Her father and her brother both played league and, later, they both refereed league. Rugby union was a totally foreign game to her. I do know that she had never watched a game of union in her life. In fact, the first union game she saw was the first one I played in after signing with the ARU — the match against the Waratahs in 2001.

Once the decision to go to union had been made and negotiations with the ARU got started, Tara became involved again. She was brought into the negotiations, which was some-thing she appreciated, because it hadn't happened to her before. She got right into the detail of the contract, and she liked the fact that the ARU people, John O'Neill and Jeff Miller, saw her as a party to the negotiations and spoke to her about it. I think this was when she really started to warm to union — she liked the attitude of the officials we were dealing with.

In 2002, Tara started attending all my Reds matches in Brisbane. She enjoyed them, even though to begin with she didn't under-stand much of what was happening on the field. One reason she enjoyed them was that she liked the atmosphere of the crowd. Tara found that rugby union crowds were just as supportive and fanatical as league crowds, and she didn't experience any foul language or an ultra-aggressive attitude to opposition players.

Over the years I'd become used to this and never thought twice about it. In any case, I was on the field, not in the grandstand. But it was a big thing with Tara, because she used to watch my matches from the grandstand with Tristan, and he was becoming old enough to take in what was said around him.

The other thing she found refreshing about union crowds was that she was hardly ever recognised as Wendell Sailor's wife. She and Tristan had become known by league fans, and every so often she'd get hassled by people who recognised her. Most of them were well-meaning, but it was still something she dreaded whenever she went to a match. At union matches, she and Tristan were just lost in the crowd.

Tara understood rugby league, so at first the fact that she knew next to nothing about the game her husband was now playing used to bother her. It didn't take her long, though, to realise that not knowing much about union wasn't really important. What mattered was that she was there at the ground, giving me support.

Tara did gradually get the hang of union. At first she used to say she was grateful I was a winger instead of, say, a backrower, because with her knowledge of league she was more or less able to understand what I was supposed to be doing. As time went on, though, she began to get a feel for the rest of the game and to understand many (but not all) of its finer points.

When I joined the Reds, Tara effectively joined, too, and it wasn't long before she began attending Reds functions and meeting other wives and girlfriends. Until she went the first time, this had worried her, because she wasn't sure what sort of reception she'd get from the other women. After all, there'd been a lot of media hype about the mega-bucks the ARU was supposed to be paying me and about how I'd been guaranteed a place in the Wallabies. This wasn't true, of course, but Tara was afraid that some of the women might believe it and that there might still be some resentment. As it turned out, she had nothing to worry about. The union women — and the players, too — couldn't have made her feel more welcome.

Because the Super 12 season is a lot shorter than the NRL season, Reds wives don't see as much of each other as Broncos' wives do. Where Tara really got to know the others well was at the Wallabies' camp at Coffs Harbour. She teamed up there with wives of the Reds in the squad and got on really well with them. All in all, Tara liked the rugby union environment because it felt somehow family-oriented. The Broncos are a family-oriented club, too, but after Alfie Langer and some other guys left, the number of Broncos' children dropped from 20 to about three.

At the rugby union gatherings there were heaps of children. I don't know if there's something about the game that makes rugby union players produce more kids, but there did seem to be two or three per player, which was great. Tara particularly liked the fact that the players' parents and the wives' parents came to the games. Everybody in the family seemed to be included, which Tara found very nice.

At the same time, Tara hasn't lost touch with her friends at the Broncos. She still keeps in close touch with the Broncos' wives and girlfriends she's friends with, and she still takes Tristan to playgroup with the Broncos' mothers. Among her close league friends are Renee Lee, wife of Phil, and Lote Tuqiri's girlfriend Rebecca. She tells me the attitude of the Broncos' wives and girlfriends to her hasn't changed one bit. It's as if I am still playing for the Broncos.

What Tara didn't get used to was the criticism, a lot of it unfair, that was heaped on me by people on both sides of the fence, league and union. Whenever she heard or read of league people attacking me for being a traitor to the game, she'd always want to jump up and write a letter to the newspapers, explaining my side of it. One point she was keen to make (which I hadn't thought of myself) is that people in the rest of the workforce change jobs without anybody thinking twice about it, so why should so many people get worked up about me changing jobs? After all, I'd been in the same job for nine years.

I'm very happy Wendell did it [switched codes]. Professionally, Wendell was at a point where he needed something else. From a family point of view I'm happy, too. With Tristan, we were ready to move into a more family-oriented environment. Rugby union is very much more that. We're not discouraged from going away with the boys. With rugby union, the boys like having you there. I remember the first day at the Coffs Harbour camp, I didn't know half the players there, but Owen Finegan came up and welcomed me and introduced me around. Before that, he didn't know who I was. They welcome the wives, they welcome the children, and I just found that so nice. They subsidise trips, they pay for air fares for children and us, and they really look after you and your children when you're there.

TARA SAILOR

Tristan seems to have settled into the rugby union environment, too. He told Tara the other day that when he grows up he's going to play for the Broncos, the Kangaroos, the Reds and the Wallabies, in that order. In other words, he wants to follow in his father's footsteps. Maybe he'll do it, too — he already loves kicking a footy around.

My advice to anyone thinking of switching codes is that they'd better make sure beforehand that they have a supportive spouse. If they don't, it will be hard going for them. If Tara hadn't been so supportive of my decision to switch to union — I was risking her future as well as my own, after all — I am sure I wouldn't have made it. The pressure on me to adjust to union and perform as the public expected me to perform gave me more than enough to worry about. If I'd also had to worry about how my wife was feeling about me switching, it would probably all have been too much.

TWO CODES:
A PLAYER'S COMPARISON

How do the two codes rate from a player's point of view? They're different, of course, and if I had to sum it up in a sentence I'd say that in union you always have to be thinking one or two steps ahead of the play. I once heard Jason Akermanis, the Brisbane Aussie Rules player, quoted as saying that rugby league is played by simple people. I don't know about league people being simple, but I do agree that league is a more simple game than union. Nothing wrong with that. In fact, this is probably why league has been so popular. All in all, I don't believe anyone would argue that union isn't a harder game mentally. Obviously, it is. There are more things going on in union and therefore more things to think about. Most of the time in league you react to what happens — you try to take advantage of each situation as it arises. In union you have to be always thinking ahead, because in union one thing always leads to another.

So union is tougher mentally than league. But is league tougher physically than union? It isn't an easy question to answer. League people believe league is a harder game than union, and I probably used to believe that myself. Having played both codes now, I can say for certain that, overall, neither code is harder than the other, although each is harder in certain ways. I'm sure Mat Rogers would say the same thing. League used to be harder mainly because the defence was tougher and there were more big hits, but defence in union is now as good as in league. Union players tackle just about as well as league players now, and that's mainly because union has adopted league techniques. All around the world, union teams have been employing league people to teach them how to tackle. When I joined the Reds we had a former league player, Trevor Gillmeister, working with us on defensive techniques.

In the second Test against France in 2002, I got hit as hard as I've ever been hit in a State of Origin match. Getting bashed by a French backrower who weighs maybe 118 kilograms and is a top athlete as well is no picnic, and I came out of it with the first stitches I've ever had in my football career. Running with the ball, I stepped back into the French forward pack and a backrower hammered me. The result: three stitches under the eye. To the best of my memory, this was the first time in my football career that I'd even been cut.

In league, the physical stuff ends as soon as you get tackled, but in union that's when the worst of the physical stuff often begins. You get shoed, kicked or trampled on while you're lying on the ground. In one of my first Super 12 matches I laid the ball back and as I did so someone stood on my hand. It was a taste of what was ahead for me. In union, you feel much more vulnerable physically. If you're anywhere near the centre of the action, boots, knees and elbows can come at you from any angle.

I'd have to say that you'll see more things go wrong in union — more mess-ups, more dropped balls, more wayward passes and so on — and this is because in union there are more things happening at any one time, so more mistakes are possible. League is a more straightforward game, which is one reason that it's so good to watch.

Where I think union has definitely got an edge on league is in general ball skills — quick hands, flick passes, aerial skills and so on. That's because union players devote a lot of their training time to practising skills, whereas league players at training do more physical work. Some league players, like Andrew Johns and Brad Fittler, do have amazing ball skills, but not everyone in league needs to have those skills. You don't need them if you're a hit-up centre. All you need is to be able to take the short ball. In union, though, centres like Tim Horan have fantastic skills. As a Bronco I used to watch him and think how brilliant he was.

On the other hand, I'd say that, across the board, league players are physically superior to union players, and this is because of league's bigger emphasis on physical work at training. (At the same time, David Croft and Chris Latham are among the fittest guys I know.) League players train much harder for fitness, which is something I really noticed when I joined the Reds. I'd estimate that my fitness work with the Reds was about half what it was with the Broncos. I know that this is one area that the Wallaby coach, Eddie Jones, wants to work on in 2003 — he wants to step up the Wallabies' physical work.

I'd also say league is a better game for running the ball, mainly because you get more opportunities to do it. Opportunities for running the ball don't come so often in union, and when they do you have two more defenders to worry about. In league, the five-tackle rule means you're going to get the ball booted to you every few minutes with a chance to counterattack, which I used to love.

In union, no matter what you do, it's often hard to get your hands on the ball, which can be frustrating. Stirling Mortlock and I talked about this. I don't know how many times I came round the back off my wing, looking for the ball, only to find the ball had gone the other way. In one Super 12 match when I went searching for the ball on the other side of the field, Ben Tune ended up scoring a try on my wing. I suppose this showed up my inexperience in union. You have to know where to be. Chris Latham and Mat Rogers are good at this. Both of them can sniff a try.

'I don't have any problem running the lines and angles, but there are so many more backline moves. And you mustn't get isolated on the wrong side of the ruck — you have to watch what side you land on when tackled. In league, I just roved and took the ball up on the edge of the ruck. Pretty simple, really.'

WENDELL SAILOR, SPEAKING TO THE MEDIA A FEW DAYS BEFORE HIS DEBUT MATCH FOR THE REDS, OCTOBER 2001.

One thing I can say for sure is that union is a more exhausting game than league. As I said before, league is a stop-start game. You get to have a bit of a rest after every tackle. In union, the play can go on and on. The phases keep rolling, and even if your legs and body are stuffed, you have to keep turning up in position. You have to be there to support the breakdown. League is strenuous in bursts. In union, the pressure on your fitness is constant.

The aerobics of union are a lot tougher than most league players realise. They're certainly a lot tougher than I realised before I began playing it. I knew it was aerobically tough for forwards, who have to follow the play wherever it goes, but it's also tough for backs — even if they're marking time out on the wing. Wingers have to go back when, as often happens, the ball is kicked behind them, and if, say, Chris Latham joins the backline, a winger has to go back and cover as fullback.

All in all, though, I'd say the two codes are about on a par as far as the players' ability is concerned. This is definitely true of the top level, which is where I've had personal experience of both. In my opinion, taken as a whole, the players of one code are about as skilled and tough and talented as the players of the other. This wasn't always true — even rugby union people will admit now that their standard of defence used to be pretty ordinary compared with league — but it is true today. The players of both codes realise this, which is why, as I said before, there is so much respect between them.

A FEW OF MY FAVOURITE UNION PEOPLE

I have found that one of the best things about being an elite footballer is that you come into close contact with the greats of your game — or, in my case, the greats of two games. I have never lost the feeling of awe that I had as a kid when I came close to a champion. In my one year or so as a full-time union professional, I've played with or against just about all the best players in the world today and most of the best players of the past decade. I'd like to write about a few of them in this chapter, not because I necessarily think they're the best players in the world (although you could argue that all of them are), but because they're players I've come across in one way or another and really admired. Here they are.

TOUTAI KEFU   Two or three years ago I was having dinner one night with Wayne Bennett and Gorden Tallis when we began talking about the union players we thought could make it to the top in league. Tim Horan and Daniel Herbert, I remember, were two people that Wayne suggested might do well, and we agreed with him. There was another player, though, who would have been at the top of Wayne's wish list of union stars — Toutai Kefu. 'I wouldn't mind having him,' Wayne said, which, coming from Wayne, was top praise.

Kefu was one of my favourite union players then, and he's an even bigger favourite of mine today, because I've not only played with him and seen him in action up close, but I've got to know him well. Toutai is one of those rare individuals who have a kind of aura about them, both on and off the field. He isn't captain of the Wallabies or even of the Reds, but in my opinion he's a natural leader. He doesn't talk a lot: he leads with his actions. He's someone you want to follow. Just seeing him sitting in the dressing room with you before a match gives you a feeling of confidence. And when you run out on the field, he's one of those blokes that you like to follow.

Before I joined the Reds, someone said to me that Kefu wasn't an easy bloke to get to know. That's not true. It's not hard to get to know Toutai: it just takes a bit of time. When you do get to know him, you find he's a rather private bloke who nevertheless enjoys a punt, a beer and a joke. While he doesn't talk much, you listen to everything he says, because you know that he means it. He's actually a good, knockabout bloke, and I've found he has a very good sense of humour. He's also a bloke who has a wide interest in sports. I've talked to him about racing, which he loves, and about boxing, rugby league, even soccer.

As a player, a forward, I rate him near the top. In fact, if I had to list the five best rugby union players in the world today, Kefu would be one of them. On the training field, he only just does enough. On the playing field, he gives everything he's got, which is why I think Gorden Tallis has so much respect for him. Toutai weighs 112 to 113 kilograms, but he has the footwork of someone half his size. He's got great skills, and he can hit as hard as anyone I've ever seen. He can even kick. He's a bit like Anthony Mundine: he can do anything. He's a handy boxer, and I believe he played basketball for the Australian under-19s.

Best of all, he's a champion bloke. When I come to the end of my rugby union career, Toutai is one of the people that I'll be proud to have played with.

MAT ROGERS Mat Rogers and I have one thing in common: we're both former league internationals who set out to become union internationals. But that's about the only thing we do have in common. Whereas I was a complete novice when I switched to union, Mat was going back to a game that he'd grown up in and that he already knew pretty well. Also, while Mat is a thinking player, I'm essentially a power player. In fact, Wayne Bennett once said that I play better when I don't think. In other words, I play better when I follow my instincts and do what comes naturally.

Still, Mat and I were pretty much in the same boat in 2002 and we kept in touch throughout the year. He'd phone me or I'd phone him and we'd compare notes and swap stories. Both of us were enjoying our new lives in union, which made the contact between us easier.

But Mat had three big advantages over me when it came to union. One, because he grew up in the game, he was able to play it instinctively once he became re-acclimatised to it, which he did pretty quickly. Two, he's a utility player — in fact, probably the best utility player in both rugby codes at the moment — and a player of his type is just what rugby union in Australia needs. Three, while he has the speed, the strength and all the other physical qualities that a top player needs, he also has a first-class football brain. He thinks on his feet. He can always tell where the opportunities are, where the holes are. I rate him one of the most elusive runners of the ball in either code. Often I watch him in a game and think how clever he is.

Mat and I have had parallel careers. We went from playing State of Origin and Tests in league together to playing Australian rugby Sevens together, playing Super 12 together, playing Australia A together, and finally playing for the Wallabies together. Mat and I aren't close mates, but we've always been good mates, and we've supported each other since we switched to union. After I was dropped from the Wallabies, Mat was sympathetic, saying he hoped I'd get back. There's never any friction between us, because even though Mat can play wing, we're not really competing for the same place in the team. Mat is a utility player, which I could never hope to be.

Anyone reading the sports pages in 2002 might have wondered whether we really were good mates. I finally came up against him on the field when we played the Waratahs in Brisbane in early May. In the days leading up to the match we had a shot at each other in the media. I said in my column in the *Courier-Mail* that it was just as well for Mat that he was playing for NSW and not Queensland, because otherwise he wouldn't get a game as fullback. I wrote, 'With no disrespect, I wouldn't be swapping Chris Latham for him. Latho is the man right now, absolutely red hot, and it's no coincidence the Reds are on a roll at the same time.' But I added, 'Full credit to Matty this season. He's taken to rugby like a duck to water. He's had a scoot, he's bounced and pirouetted out of tackles, he's stepped left and right and he's proved his toughness.'

Mat left a message on my phone saying, 'What's this about

Rugby's new recruit: Sailor after the announcement that he was switching to union and joining the Reds (*AAP Image/Dave Hunt*)

Queensland's captain, John Eales, welcomes Sailor to the Reds
(*AAP Image/Dave Hunt*)

Sailor is grabbed in front and from behind at the first State of Origin in 2001, which Queensland won, 34 to 16 (*AAP Image/Dave Hunt*)

A victory kiss from son Tristan after Queensland thrashed NSW 40-14 in the third State of Origin in 2001 (*AAP Image/Dave Hunt*)

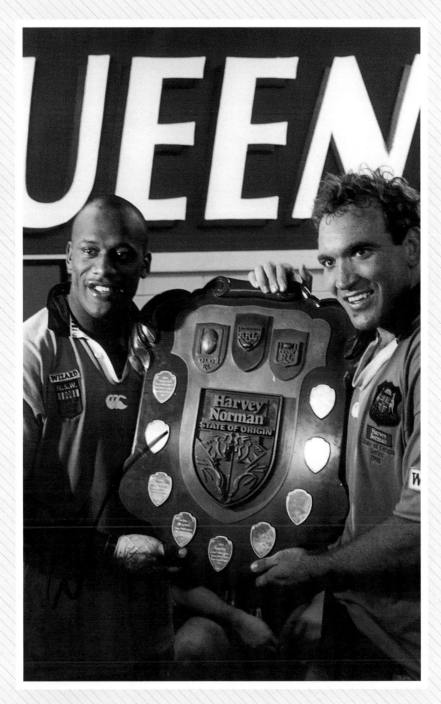

State of Origin victors – Sailor and Gorden Tallis
(Sailor Family collection)

The Kangaroos assemble for a photo shoot at Wellington before their one-off Test against New Zealand in July 2001. Bryan Fletcher is on Sailor's right and Petero Civoniceva on his left *(AAP Image/Dean Lewins)*

Sailor on a rampaging run for the Kangaroos against New Zealand in Wellington, July 2001 *(AAP Image/Sandra Teddy/Photosport)*

Sailor does a publicity shot before his first training session with the Reds, October 2001 (*AAP Image/Dave Hunt*)

Sailor at his first training session with the Reds, October 2001 (*AAP Image/Dave Hunt*)

Sailor gets plenty of attention during his first game for the Reds – against the Waratahs in October 2001 (*AAP Image/Dave Hunt*)

Sailor off the tee at the Jack Newton Celebrity Classic at the Sunshine Coast in December 2001. Golf is his favourite relaxation (*AAP Image/Dave Hunt*)

Sailor with the Australian Sevens captain, Richard Graham, in the lead-up to the international World Rugby Sevens tournament at Brisbane, February 2002 (*AAP Image/Dave Hunt*)

All smiles at training a couple of days before the World Rugby Sevens tournament in February 2002. Sailor (in the hat) was about to make his first appearance for Australia as a union player *(AAP Image/Dave Hunt)*

Sailor wore distinctive headgear at training a couple of days before the international World Rugby Sevens tournament at Brisbane, February 2002 *(AAP Image/Dave Hunt)*

Not a try. Sailor crosses the line against Papua New Guinea in the World Rugby Sevens tournament at Brisbane, February 2002 – but the try was disallowed (*AAP Image/Dave Hunt*)

Sailor keeps a Samoan defender at arm's length during the World Rugby Sevens tournament at Brisbane, February 2002 *(AAP Image/Dave Hunt)*

Rugby's latest recruits, Sailor and Mat Rogers, enjoy Australia's World Sevens win in 2001*(Sailor Family collection)*

The Reds' latest recruit inspects his new jersey at the official launch of the 2002 season (*AAP Image/Vera Devai*)

Sailor scrambles past Jorrie Muller in the Super 12 match against the Cats at Ellis Park, Johannesburg, in April 2002 (*AAP Image/Africa Visuals*)

Sailor powers through for Australia A against Canada in June 2002. Sailor scored two tries in this match (*AAP Image/Dean Lewins*)

Sailor's first try as a Wallaby – against New Zealand Maori at Perth in June 2002
(*AAP Image/Andy Tyndall*)

Hard at work in the second Test against France
(*Action Photographics*)

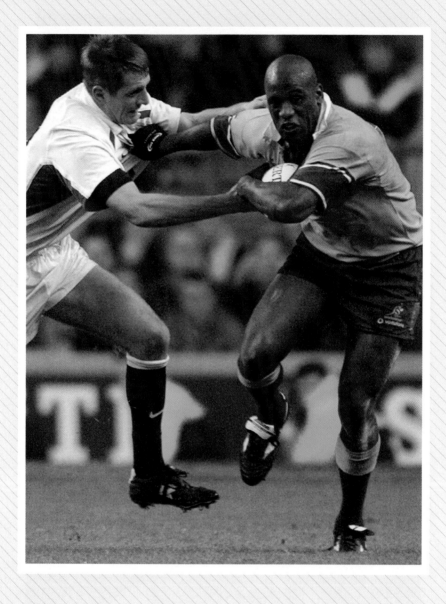

England's Ben Cohen clings desperately to Sailor during the Test at Twickenham, November 2002. Sailor rates this his second-best performance in 2002
(*AP Photo/Alastair Grant/AAP Image*)

Sailor and Cathy Freeman. Each is a fan of the other
(*Sailor Family collection*)

Two Queenslanders: Sailor and Pat Rafter
(Courier-Mail/David Kapernick)

you stitching me up in your column? What's going on, mate?' He was laughing when he said it, but then he came back at me in his own column in the *Sun-Herald* on the day of the match, a Sunday. He thanked me for motivating him with my comments about him not rating with Latham, and he talked about how many times he was going to run around me. It was all harmless fun, although I wasn't really in the mood for fun that day. The day before, I'd got involved in the 'road rage' incident.

Did he run around me in that Waratahs match as he promised he would? Not as far as I can remember. In fact, I don't think we really came in contact with each other on the field. By his own standards, Mat didn't have a great game that day. It was a big match for him, just as it was for me, and he was frustrated, because he only touched the ball two or three times in the whole game. His next game for the Waratahs wasn't much better. They got thrashed by the Crusaders, and Mat was injured and had to leave the field. I said to him afterwards, 'Hey, what about you blokes against the Crusaders?' He said, 'When I was on the field it was only three–nil.' I came back, 'Mat, that doesn't count. You have to go down with the ship, mate.'

I was really happy for Mat when he scored a try against the All Blacks. I sent him a text message saying well done, and he sent me one back saying thanks.

JASON ROBINSON After my first rugby season in Australia was over, a journalist asked me who in my opinion were the best running backs in league and union, meaning the players best able to break the line. After thinking for a minute, I said that in league, provided they were on song, the best running backs were Lote Tuqiri and Chris Walker. Both are fantastic runners of the ball — Chris Walker's ability to break the line is uncanny — and I couldn't separate them. They can either beat defenders with their strength or go through holes. Both of them always know if there's a hole anywhere.

As far as union is concerned, I didn't have to think for even a minute before choosing Jason Robinson of England. I'd put Mat Rogers only a fraction behind him. Robinson is one of the players I admire most in both codes. I've always been amazed at his ability to find a gap in the defence and slip through it. I've watched him doing it over and over on tape, and I still don't quite know how he does it. English rugby made a very, very valuable signing when he decided to switch from league.

JONAH LOMU What a player! In my Bronco days I used to watch him and think what a sensation he'd be if he ever switched to league. As it turned out, I was the one that switched, and I started to have Jonah's name thrown up at me even before I went over to union. When I played in the league Test at Wellington in 2001, people in the crowd called out to me: 'Hey Sailor, how do you think you'll go against Jonah?' or 'Just wait until you play against Jonah, Sailor — he's going to smash you.' Then, when we went out for a few beers after the game, people kept coming up to me saying the same thing.

There was a lot of media hype before the Reds played Jonah's team, the Hurricanes, in 2002. It was supposed to be a one-on-one clash between me and him, but this was never going to happen because we were on opposite wings. Ben Tune was on Jonah's wing, and a few days before the match Ben said, as a joke, that I could mark Jonah if I wanted to. As it turned out, Jonah and I didn't even make contact on the field. I roved over to his wing a few times and he roved over to mine, but we never ended up in a one-on-one situation. So, as far as the media was concerned, the whole occasion was probably a bit of a let-down.

We met each other once a few years ago at some promotion. Jonah said to me that he'd watched me play in a couple of rugby league Tests, and I told him I'd often watched him when the All Blacks were playing. There was mutual respect, and in professional sport mutual respect makes the world go round. Before the Hurricanes match, I asked Daniel Herbert, 'How quick's Jonah?' He said, 'Well, put it this way: you're about the quickest here. Jonah probably weighs 10 kilograms more than you weigh and he's still quicker than you.'

My only contact with Jonah when we played the Hurricanes was when we shook hands after the match. He said, 'How you going?' and I said, 'Good.' That was all. But I felt that as we shook hands we were exchanging mutual respect. He had a great game that day, incidentally, as I had suspected he would, because he'd been off touch before.

He's one of those players who have something special about them. Maybe you could call it star quality. I could count the number of players who have it, both in league and union, on one hand. The first time I saw much of him was during union's 1995 World Cup. Like the other Broncos who watched him then, I couldn't believe the way he tore teams apart.

I had no illusions about Jonah. Anyone who weighs nearly 120 kilograms, as he does, and travels as fast as he travels must be hard to stop. I admire him as a great athlete and I like him as a person.

GEORGE GREGAN After I was picked in the Wallaby squad there was a media function at Darling Harbour in Sydney which I attended with the other Wallabies. We went there in a boat, and this was the first time I'd had a chance to have a good yarn with Georgie Gregan. As we all know, George isn't a big guy physically, but he does have a big presence about him. As I talked to him that day I felt a bit overawed, which I suppose was silly for someone like me, who'd been mixing with top footballers since the age of 18. But that's the effect George had on me, and I think he has it on other players, too. It's one of the reasons he's such a good leader as well as being such a good competitor and such a good player.

George is without doubt the most professional footballer I've come in contact with. Somehow, he seems to do everything just right. He trains right. He eats right. He sleeps right. His physique is right. He even drinks right. He'll have a few beers with the boys then go to bed. Eddie Jones said to me once that I could learn a lot from George in how to manage myself. The trouble is, I'm a different personality altogether from George. I'm not one to have a few beers with my team-mates and go to bed. In fact, I enjoy having a drink, even with players from opposition teams.

I appreciated all the help George gave me in 2002. From the day I joined the Wallabies he kept encouraging me and reassuring me that I was on track with my game. He let me know that I was wanted in the Wallabies. After training, he'd be the first to invite me to join him and a few others for a meal in a restaurant. He made me feel I fitted in, and I will always be grateful to him for that.

I won't be grateful to him for stripping that ball from me in the first Super 12 match of the season, though. I still look back on that moment and think how different things might have been if I'd scored a try in that match. If George hadn't stripped the ball from me, I would have been spared nearly two months of grief while everyone — including me — waited for me to score my first Super 12 try. Stripping the ball wasn't a fluke. I have discovered since that George does have a knack of whacking the ball out of your hands, either from above or below. He did it again to me at one of our Wallaby training sessions. I said to him, 'Mate, do you realise you put about nine weeks of pressure on me by doing that?' He more than made up for it, though, with the personal support he gave me later in the season.

LEAGUE VERSUS UNION?

Personally, I have never wanted to think of league and union in terms of one versus the other. In my opinion, people who do think of them this way are small-minded: they're thinking within the square. They need to start thinking outside the square and recognise that the two rugby codes are both part of the overall sports scene. For one to do well, you don't need the other to do badly.

The basic problem with people who like to see league and union this way is that they think there's room for only one rugby code and that, therefore, one has to somehow beat the other. Again, this is small-minded. Would union really be better off if league died tomorrow? I doubt it. I once heard a league official say that in his opinion the last thing union people would want is for league to die and all its supporters move across to rugby. He was having a shot at union, meaning that the toffs who follow union wouldn't want to mix with the league hoons, but I actually think there was some truth in what he said, although not in the way he meant it. I believe union supporters would hate to have the culture of their game changed because they were suddenly swamped by league followers.

While I think there's definitely room for the two successful rugby codes in Australia, I do also believe that they will always compete with each other. I don't see them getting together — at least not in the next 10 to 15 years. The hierarchies of the two codes are too far apart. And although the players of the two codes respect each other and watch each other's games, there's still rivalry between them. It may be friendly rivalry, but it's still rivalry.

I know the rugby union boys get a bit dirty at Gorden Tallis when he comes out with another shot at union. Gorden once suggested that the Wallabies and the Kangaroos should decide which was the better team by playing each other under hybrid rules. I know Gorden is passionate about league, but I really think comments like that are schoolboy stuff. The point is, that's the way a lot of league people think.

Union players sometimes have a shot at league, too, even if they don't often do it in public. They call league players 'mungos' in the same way that league players called union players 'rah-rahs', and I've heard the union boys talking among themselves about the fact that 'there are more mungos coming over'. I think the term 'mungo', which has been around for a few years, probably originated in the days when union players were still amateurs and looked down on league players as working-class professionals.

Since switching to union and being able to see things from both sides, I've often wished that more league people could open their minds and see how good Super 12 and international union can be, and I've often wished that more union people could recognise what a terrific event the State of Origin is.

I know the Wallabies think it's a terrific event. In the week before the Test against France in Sydney in 2002, 13 or 14 blokes from the Wallaby team — me included — went to watch the State of Origin in Sydney from the ARU's corporate box. Bernie Larkham, Ben Tune and Justin Harrison were three of those there, I remember. The atmosphere was electric, and the Wallabies talked about this among themselves, saying how awesome it was. I sat there thinking how much things had changed for me: the year before I'd been down there on the field, playing in this same game, and here I was now, sitting in the grandstand in a Wallaby blazer and preparing to play in a union Test the following Saturday.

I'm stating the obvious by saying that union has it all over league at the international level. On the other hand, league is tremendously strong at the grassroots level in NSW and Queensland, which is why it turns out so many talented players. League players are not only getting better — they're also getting younger. The other day I met Brett Seymour, a new and talented Bronco, who, incidentally, went to the same school I did at Mackay — St Patrick's. He's only 17, but he has all the skills and all the confidence in the world already.

There are others just like him coming through, because league is identifying the talent earlier and earlier. Rugby union is aware of this, and I was interested to see an ARU official quoted recently as saying that young league players were up to four years further advanced, physically, than union players of the same age. Eddie Jones once said much the same thing to me: that when he went to Parramatta a couple of years ago he noticed that the young league players were physically more built up than their equivalents in union. They had six-packs and were carrying a lot of muscle.

I'd agree with all this, but there is a down side to bringing players through younger. A question I sometimes get asked is: why do league players seem to get into more trouble off the field than union players? I think the answer in most cases is simple: it has to do with the fact that league players tend to make it to the top younger. If a league player is talented enough, he leaves school and doesn't go to university or TAFE because he has already started playing first grade at the age of 18 or 19. He's happy to become a professional footballer.

If he makes it, he's soon earning $150,000 to $200,000 a year, which is a lot of money for a kid to handle if he's come from a working-class background and hasn't had any experience of handling money. So this young league player, maybe 18 or 19 or 20 years old, looks around and thinks what a great life this is. The clubs are throwing big money at him, and he's getting a high profile in the media. People recognise him in restaurants. Suddenly, he has fame and fortune, and he thinks nothing can stop him, that he's on top of the world. And he's still maybe only 19. No wonder he cuts loose every so often.

This is where I believe that league clubs have generally fallen down: they have paid their young players all this money, but they've done very little to advise them on how to handle it — and how to handle life when you're earning so much. Wayne Bennett gave a lead here which I hope all league clubs will follow. He began getting in financial advisers, career advisers and so on. When I switched codes I found that union provided this type of advice to players, which I thought was pretty impressive, considering union has been professional for only six or seven years. After I moved to union, expert advisers were laid on to help me make the right decisions about the kind of career I want after I retire as a player and to advise me on how to set up that career. Others offered investment advice.

The main reason league players are brought on so young is that league's talent identification is very good. Take my own case. I first came to Wayne Bennett's notice when I was only 16. Wayne told me this one evening at dinner in England in 1997, the year we went over there for the world club challenge. He said he saw me play for North Queensland under-17s in the state league. The reason he came to see me was that the Broncos' recruitment manager, Cyril Connell, had told him I was a player of potential who was worth watching. Cyril is a legend in the club for travelling around and discovering talent in the country. Anyway, according to Wayne, I did some good things on the field that day but then I'd go back on my wing and take it easy. He thought I was lazy and marked me down as a player lacking work ethic.

(Funnily enough, Wayne thought the same of Gorden Tallis when he saw him play as a 16-year-old. He had met Gorden a couple of years before this. Wayne had signed on Gorden's older brother, Wally, and somewhere — maybe at the Tallis home — he met young Gorden, who was cheeky enough to say to him that he had signed the wrong brother. 'I'm going to play for the Broncos,' Gorden said. Wayne told the boy he liked his confidence, but when he saw him play a couple of years later he thought he was lazy. Wayne told us at dinner that night that he was wrong about both of us: he let Gorden go to St George because he didn't want to sign him, and he didn't want to sign me either. It was only after he saw me play for St Patrick's College in a Catholic schools tournament in Brisbane, where I scored a swag of tries, that he decided I was worth having.)

When I joined the Reds there weren't any 18-year-olds or 19-year-olds in the team. Blokes of that age were still in the B team. I referred before to Brett Seymour. If you look at the Broncos, you'll also see quite a few 19-year-olds and 20-year-olds coming through and playing first grade. In union, these same players would probably make it around 23 or 24 — or maybe not until 25 or 26. So when these union players start earning big money they're a lot more mature and have enough experience and common sense to cope with their fame and fortune (not to mention the help they get with it all from the ARU). Chances are they also have some type of qualification, maybe a university degree: they have a career planned for after football and they're already working towards it. All in all, they have their heads screwed on better and can see their 'fame and fortune' in perspective. Blokes like this are less likely to run wild and disgrace themselves.

After leaving school I set out to become a policeman, and when I joined the Broncos as an 18-year-old I was enrolled at the police academy at Kangaroo Point in Brisbane. I'd finished about the first six months of the course when I was picked to play first grade. Before that, I'd been on a junior contract with the Broncos. I was given free board and lodging plus $100 a week, and at the time I thought I was doing well. Then I moved up to first grade, and suddenly I was paid $1500 a week. I'll never forget pocketing my first week's pay. I was 18 years old and I had $1500 in my wallet, with another $1500 to come the next week and $1500 every week after that. I felt as if I'd won Lotto.

What did I do with it? I splurged on cars. I bought three cars within 12 months, which was pretty stupid. I did send a few hundred dollars to my parents each week, and I also got bitten by people wanting a loan. If they didn't phone me directly, they'd phone my mother and ask her if she could ask me if I'd lend them a couple of thousand dollars or whatever. I did lend money to some of these relatives, and a few of them never paid me back. The same thing had happened to my father, so I knew then how he felt.

This would never — or hardly ever — happen in union. I'm told Tim Horan had only just turned 19 when he made his debut for the Wallabies, but he'd be a rare exception. Most union players don't make it big until they're mature, so there's a different culture. Blokes are expected to behave themselves and be responsible, and even if an 18-year-old gets to the top early in union he'll probably fall into line with this and not let the money go to his head. League doesn't have that culture. That's how I see the situation, anyway.

To get back to the subject of competition between the two codes: my view is that there's not only plenty of room for both codes but that each can benefit by feeding off the other to some extent. The fact that there are two codes means people have a choice. You can follow both codes or you can follow the one you like better. What I have found since switching to union is that a lot of people are interested in the differences between the two codes — and there are plenty of these differences, off the field as well as on.

For example, I've been asked whether union players socialise more than league players. Many people seem to believe that they do. I once read somewhere that when Michael O'Connor crossed from league to union in the early 1980s he found there was less socialising after training and after matches in league than in union. The idea was that the league boys saw football as their job and, like a lot of blokes, they didn't go out socialising with their workmates when work was over: they'd go home or get together with their close friends. Union was supposed to be different because it was still just a game to the people who played it, so naturally they'd socialise more.

I don't doubt this was true when O'Connor went over to league, but now that rugby has gone professional I don't see much difference between the codes in how much socialising the boys do after they finish training or playing. In fact, I've never known any group of footballers to be closer than the Broncos.

Where I do see a difference is the type of socialising they do. League players generally go out on the town more than union players. When I first started playing league in Brisbane, players would head off to the bars and nightclubs as soon as a game was over and spend the night drinking. There's not so much of this now as there was 10 years ago, but it's still the custom. The Broncos' motto is still 'Train hard, play hard, drink hard.' As I've said elsewhere, Wayne Bennett encouraged this. I remember after we lost four games straight in 2001, Wayne said mid-week, 'Boys, just go out and have a drink and unwind.'

Union players like to unwind after a match, too, but they do it more in-house. They're happy to sit around the hotel and have a few drinking games or go to a restaurant for dinner.

I think Wayne Bennett set the right example, not only for league people but also for union people, in how to deal with the other code. Nobody could be more loyal to league than Wayne, but I always found he had a completely open mind as far as union was concerned. He didn't have a set against it, as some league people do. A good example of that was how he reacted when I wanted to switch to union. He didn't want me to go and tried to talk me out of it, but once he saw my mind was made up he wished me all the best and helped me where he could. In fact, he has continued to help me with advice right up to the present.

Eddie Jones is the same. I remember standing next to the team bus one day and talking to him about league and league players.

I was surprised at how much he knew about them. He'd sized up the league players in detail, which meant he must have studied the game pretty closely.

It was because Wayne Bennett was so open-minded about union that I was able to return to the Broncos once a week towards the end of the 2002 season and train with them. A lot of coaches would have had a grudge against a player like me who had left to go to the other code and probably wouldn't have let me near the place. Wayne is different. I was aware that another old Bronco, Peter Ryan, had gone back to do pre-season training with the Broncos before rejoining the Brumbies, so I asked Benny if I could do the same thing. Benny said, 'Mate, you're welcome any time. It's still your home.'

The training was part of my Wallaby program, so I also had to get the okay from Eddie Jones. I spoke to him about my training program and he asked me what I was doing. I told him I'd be boxing one day a week with my personal trainer, Mark Burgess, and doing some sprints, and then I said, 'But I wouldn't mind going back to the Broncos once a week and training with them.' Eddie replied, 'I'm more than happy for you to do that.' So in my official Wallaby training schedule, there was an unusual entry: 'Training with the Broncos.'

MY WISH LIST
OF RECRUITS FROM
LEAGUE

How do I compare union and league players? If they're forwards, I wouldn't try. Their roles are so different that comparisons are impossible. To compare Toutai Kefu with Gorden Tallis would be like comparing a golfer with a cricketer. Can anyone imagine a league front-rower packing down in a union scrum? He'd have his neck broken. At the same time, some union forwards could not play the way league forwards play. Nick Stiles could not do what Shane Webcke does — and vice versa. I happen to know, incidentally, that Nick has a lot of respect for the way Shane plays.

Having played both codes, I feel I'm on safe ground choosing a few league people who could make it, big-time, in union. This doesn't mean necessarily that I rate them the best players in league. Gorden Tallis isn't in the list, for example. They're just the players who have that particular blend of physique and skills that, in my opinion, would get them to the top in union. Plus, as you will see, a coach.

Here, in no particular order, is my list.

ANDREW JOHNS I honestly believe that Andrew Johns could be the best player in both codes. In my opinion he's already the best player in league, and if he came across to union I'm pretty sure he'd be union's best player, too — if not the best, one of the best. Apart from his skills, he's just so tough. At first glance you might think he's just a little fat bloke, but he's actually a ball of muscle, a nugget. His football skills are unbelievable. The union boys really admire him. I've heard them say, 'Andrew Johns — what a player!'

In union, I could see Johns playing either halfback or five-eighth. His passing (both sides) is fantastic, he can draw a player better than anyone I know, he's got great vision, he can kick the ball, both feet, anywhere he wants, just like Andrew Mehrtens, and he hits as hard as Gorden Tallis in defence. He also has an amazing football brain. If the Broncos were playing the Knights and I was running with the ball, I'd hear him call to his defenders, 'Sailor's got a left-foot step, watch his left-foot step, watch his left-foot step, left right, left right.' He's one of those players who are so good they make you feel second-rate. I'd watch Johns in action and I'd think to myself, 'What am I doing out here?'

DARREN LOCKYER He could play fullback or five-eighth in union. Whatever he does, he has all the time in the world, which in my opinion is a sign of real class. He's always a step ahead of everyone else on the field: he's got terrific vision, just like Stephen Larkham. He has a great boot, too. He can put the ball anywhere he likes with either foot, and, of course, he's a wonderful runner of the ball. In his case, I'd call it gliding rather than running. I've always had the impression that Darren can run as fast laterally as he can straight ahead. Also, he's very tough.

TRENT BARRETT He's another that has great vision — he's always one step ahead of the game. He's a top runner of the ball, he's good in defence, he can pass both sides and kick both feet, and he's a good leader. He's definitely a player I think could adapt successfully to union. I'd rate him as one of the three best players in league at the moment. The others are Andrew Johns and Darren Lockyer. It's no coincidence that these also happen to be three of the players I think could make it in union, because I believe a top-class back in either code could make it in the other.

PETERO CIVONICEVA League forwards would obviously find it a lot harder than backs to transfer to union, and most would really struggle to do well in tight-five positions, especially the front row. Petero is an exception. I really think he would be capable of becoming a union forward — probably a backrower of some type — because it's always seemed to me that he's built for it and that he plays league like a union forward. At 192 centimetres in height and weighing 106 kilograms, he mightn't be as big as top union backrowers like Owen Finegan, but he's big enough. Why do I say he plays like a union forward? It's the way he powers through defenders with the ball in hand. Watch how he does it the next time you see him play. When he hits the line, he drops his head, lowers his body height, keeps moving and somehow comes through the other side — just like a union backrower. Maybe that's because he has a background in union. I'm told his father was a Fijian international.

LOTE TUQIRI I once heard two people talking on the radio about which was the most valuable signing of a league player that the ARU had made. One thought it was Mat Rogers.

The other thought it was me. They were both wrong. The most valuable signing so far, without doubt, is Lote Tuqiri. I'm 28. Mat Rogers is 27. Lote was only 22 when they signed him, although he's turned 23 since. He has a whole career as a Wallaby ahead of him. Lote is a special talent. He combines the best of Mat Rogers and me. He has size, speed and power, but he also has skill and flair. On top of that he has another level of performance he can rise to that is all his own.

I'm including him in my wish list of league recruits because, as I write this, he's still a league player — just. Eddie Jones asked me about him. I said, 'Mate, he's worth whatever you can afford to pay for him.' I told Eddie that Lote would be a fantastic acquisition for rugby union. In fact, Lote was on my wish list before he decided to come across to union. Before it was suggested Lote might switch, I used to think that he was destined to be the next superstar of rugby league. He has the physique, he has the speed and he has the skill, but the thing about him that really stands out is his ability to make things happen. As soon as he gets the ball in his hands, you sit up and watch, because he's liable to do something exciting. He's like David Campese in that respect. Lote is creative, flamboyant and talented. He's a good kicker — and a goal-kicker, too. The important thing is he grew up playing union. I believe he played union until he was 16, so he'll have no trouble at all switching back. In union he could play centre, wing or fullback.

Like me, Lote plays best when he doesn't think too much. He had a few ordinary games for the Broncos after he signed to switch to union, and I know (because I talked to him about it) that this was because he was thinking too much — he was trying to please too many people.

BRAITH ANASTA   He's tough, and on the field he looks to have plenty of time to do things. He has all-round skills and his defence is good. What a talent for someone so young! I'm told he played golf in the off-season and shot three under off the stick, so he's probably capable of anything. He has the confidence and the personality to go with the talent, too. You don't often see so much self-confidence in someone so young. He's destined to make it in league, and I've no doubt he'd be a star in union, too, probably as a five-eighth or centre.

WAYNE BENNETT   A lot of people, including Wayne himself, will be surprised that I have included him in this list. I'm not suggesting there's even a 1 per cent chance he'd ever want to go across and coach rugby union. In any case, rugby union probably wouldn't want him, since he's had no hands-on experience of the game. But I have so much respect for Benny's ability to get footballers to play at their best that I honestly believe that if he put his mind to it, he could be a great coach in union — as well as a great coach in soccer, Aussie Rules, hockey and just about every other sport, for that matter.

I've already had a lot to say about Wayne Bennett in this book, so I won't add more here apart from saying that he was the most outstanding personality I ever met in rugby league — a great coach, a great mentor, a great man. This isn't to say that he and I always saw eye to eye. I had a number of run-ins with him over the years, and generally it turned out that he was right and I was wrong.

I find it interesting how many players who are not part of the Broncos say they would like to be coached by Wayne Bennett. Andrew Johns almost went to the Broncos a few years ago, and

I'm sure the prospect of being coached by Wayne Bennett was one of the things that attracted him. Maybe it was the main thing. Plenty of other players from other league clubs have said to me how much they'd like to be coached by Benny. I've even had a few rugby union players say it to me. I seem to recall that Chris Latham and Nick Stiles said they'd like to be coached by Wayne. I've heard George Gregan speak highly of him, too.

I once said to Benny, 'Mate, when are you going to give it away? You're still bringing guys through and getting the best out of them, but you can't go on forever.' Wayne's reply was typical. He said, 'Wendell, I want you to go home and think about it, and then come back and tell me when you reckon I should give it away.' I did think about it and when I next saw him I said, 'Benny, I've been with you nine years now, and you're still getting the best out of me. If you can get the best out of me I'm pretty sure you can get the best out of anyone. So my advice is to keep going as long as you feel like it.'

I hope he takes that advice.

SHAKEN UP
BY EDDIE JONES

I was very fortunate to play under two outstanding coaches in my first year in rugby union — Mark McBain and Eddie Jones. Both were amazingly helpful to me at a time when I was still learning the game; both gave me plenty of encouragement to keep at it when for a while it seemed I wasn't making much headway, and both were willing to make allowances for the fact that I was new to the game and liable to make the odd mistake. As I've said before, Eddie Jones reminded me of Wayne Bennett in a number of ways. Eddie is an authoritative coach. He tells you what he wants, and what he wants is what you do. Like all good coaches, he gets to know you and works out your personality, and he uses this to get the best out of you. This is probably why he seems to have the ability to lift a player to a higher level of performance, just as Wayne Bennett does.

Also like Wayne, Eddie has the respect of the players, which, in my opinion, is the most important attribute a coach can have. And although he's an authoritative coach, Eddie does consult a lot with his senior players — guys like George Gregan, Owen Finegan and Toutai Kefu — and works with them and through them.

Wayne Bennett did exactly the same. I've described before how he'd regularly pull in his panel of 'consultants' — Gorden Tallis, Darren Lockyer, Shane Webcke and myself — and ask what we thought the team ought to be doing. This is a very smart thing for a coach to do. I think it's the only way a coach can survive in his job for any period. Coaches who believe that their way is the only way (whether or not it's the right way) never last long. Eddie is very good at handling the media, too; he may be one up on Wayne in that respect. Eddie can work the media to the team's advantage. Benny prefers to avoid the media if he can.

Like every other successful coach, Wayne Bennett plays mind games with his players to get the best out of them. Eddie Jones is the same. For example, Eddie likes everyone in the Wallaby squad to compete with each other at training. With him, you can't just turn up for training and cruise through it. You have to have a 'you-or-me' attitude to the other players.

I once ran foul of Eddie over this. It was not long after the first Bledisloe Cup match in 2002. I'd been dropped from the Wallaby team, but I was still in the Wallaby squad, and I came to training one day after getting a cortisone injection in my knee — this knee had been troubling me for a couple of years. I also wasn't as aerobically fit as I should have been. I'd been doing a lot of weights for strength, but because we didn't do as much compulsory fitness training as I'd done in the Broncos I'd become a bit complacent, maybe a bit too comfortable. Eddie Jones had earlier said to me, 'You've had a sound season, but I think you've played within yourself.' That's what I felt, myself: I knew I could have done better.

I was also feeling unhappy about being dropped. I knew it was going to happen — I knew that Ben Tune would go back on the right wing as soon as he was fit to play. That didn't bother me.

What bothered me was the way the media made it an issue when it wasn't an issue at all, when blind Freddy could see that Ben would replace me. Eddie spoke to me about it, warning me that the media would try to make a big thing about my being dropped. In fact, I would say that the media's scrutiny of everything I did was one of the things I found hardest to cope with in 2002. Take those two tackles I missed in the second Test against France. I don't deny they were bad misses, but before that I had missed only two tackles in the whole of the Super 12 season. If anyone else but me had missed the two tackles in the French Test, not nearly as much would have been made of it. I spoke to Wayne Bennett about it afterwards and told him how frustrated I felt at having every mistake spotlighted. 'You know why they do it?' he said. 'Because you're Wendell Sailor.'

But to get back to my story about Eddie Jones: Eddie had spoken to me a week or so earlier about my weight, which was then 108 to 109 kilograms. He asked me what my weight was when I was playing with the Broncos. I told him about 106 kilograms, and he said, 'Mate, I want you back to that. Your strength's fine, but your speed's down.' As far as I knew, I was still the quickest of the Wallabies, but it was true that I could be faster. Eddie said, 'Del, I want you faster and stronger.'

So over the next week, in spite of my bad knee, I trained about as hard as I ever had. I trained on at least five of the seven days. I boxed. I did a six-kilometre run with a mate. I also did a five-kilometre run. When I returned to the Wallaby camp I was down to just over 106 kilograms. Now if you drop a ball at training with the Wallabies, or throw a bad pass, or miss a tackle, you have to run around the bollards on the field. On this day I made all three mistakes, so I had to run around the bollards three times. I was feeling pretty frustrated. I was also pretty exhausted. I'd been really pumped up to train hard that day, because I was determined to leave nobody in any doubt that I was keen to get back into the team, and I'd used up just about everything in the tank.

When training was over, I was walking to the showers to have a hot and cold when Eddie pulled me aside and said, 'Del, what do you think you're doing?' I was standing there without a shirt on, wondering what he was talking about. I asked him what he meant. He said, 'What was that out there?' I said, 'Eddie, I'm disappointed with myself — that was an ordinary session for me.' He came back: 'Ordinary! Del, don't you want to be here or something?' That touched a raw nerve, and I came back strong. I told Eddie that in spite of a sore knee I'd been training my backside off to lose a few kilos in the hope of getting back into the team. 'There's no question I want to be in this team,' I said. 'I'm filthy at being dropped. I know Tuney has to go in, but I want to be in the 22 somewhere.' Eddie said, 'Okay, Del. I just wanted to know that you want to be here, and I don't want to see that out there again.' I said to him, 'Eddie, that's about as bad as you'll see from me. I'm filthy myself with that session, and I just want to leave it out there. Next week I'll be back to where I need to be.'

As I read it at the time, Eddie was suggesting that I'd been slacking, spitting the dummy out of frustration at being dropped. This wasn't true. What had happened was that I'd been carrying my knee injury since it flared up. At training that day I sprinted against Matty Burke, and I didn't stretch out because of the knee. There's not much between Matty and me in speed, but I'm reckoned to have a bit of an edge on him, so Eddie would have expected me to be ahead. When he saw I wasn't, he took this to mean I hadn't been competing hard enough, and, as I said before, Eddie puts a lot of emphasis on competing at training.

Thinking back on it later, I began to think that Eddie may have been playing a mind game with me. I do know he rides a few of the Wallabies hard to get the best out of them, and he was riding me hard that day. Wayne Bennett did the same thing for the same reason. Wayne used to ride Gorden Tallis and Chris Walker hard, for example. He used to ride me hard every so often, too. 'You're training terrible,' he'd say to me, and I'd always tell him not to worry, that I'd be right on the day.

I asked around among some of the other Wallabies, and they agreed with my idea that Eddie Jones may have taken aim at me that day to keep me keen and motivated and to get me to work harder on my fitness. It all has to do with mental toughness. You ride a player hard knowing that he'll be mentally tougher as a result. There are some personalities in the team that Eddie couldn't use this approach with, though, because it would have a negative effect.

That was my first — and so far only — run-in with Eddie, and it shook me up at the time, because I couldn't believe that anyone would think I wasn't desperate to get back into the team. As I said to Eddie later, 'I may get filthy sometimes over different things, but what I do best is play football, and I love being in this squad. Kicking cans isn't my go.' But Eddie was probably right. Maybe I needed a bit of a shake-up just at that time. When I sat down later and analysed my first season in rugby union, I realised that I had started to lose some of the work ethic that I always had at the Broncos. This was because I'd concentrated on mastering the skills and techniques of union, knowing I'd be on centre stage and that people would nitpick over everything I did; the result was that I didn't do enough physical work. I admit that now.

Eddie Jones made the point to me: 2003 is going to be a huge year for Australian rugby, and there'll be a premium on every Wallaby jersey. What I'm determined to do is get back to the body weight and the level of fitness I had at the Broncos. A mistake I made when I switched to union was to bulk up at the expense of my speed. I knew I'd be up against huge backrowers — bigger men than I'd ever had to get past in league — and I decided I needed to be bigger. I wanted to be 109 or 110 kilograms, even if that meant I wouldn't be quite as quick as I had been. So I did a lot more weights and bulked up, and I did lose a bit of speed. I suppose I had at the back of my mind, too, the idea that union players don't do as much physical training as league players, so I could afford to ease off on the physical work a little.

That was my big mistake: I didn't respect rugby union enough to realise that I still had to do the hard physical work. There were four keys to my success in league — my size, my strength, my mental toughness and my speed — and each of them was essential. By not doing the physical work, I was giving up on the last of them, my speed, which is the message that Eddie Jones was getting across to me. That's what I set about rectifying in the last few months of 2002.

TRIALS OF A CONVERT

Do I enjoy playing rugby union? It's a question I ought to answer, because during my first year in union it was suggested that I didn't look as if I was having a good time. Gorden Tallis said this on television. Referring to me, he said, 'You can tell from his body language that he's not enjoying it as much as he probably would have [liked to],' Tallis said. 'He was a wonderful rugby league player, and he was getting every accolade. If they [union people] keep on signing all these league wingers, it means they might have different plans [for Sailor]. I'm sure rugby league would open their arms for Wendell. Don't be surprised if we see him back, that's for sure.'

The next thing was that the Broncos' chief executive, Shane Edwards, picked up on Gorden's comment. 'Wendell is always welcome back here,' Shane was quoted as saying. 'He knows that. If he ever does [want to come back], we'll certainly be sitting down and talking to him.' Shane had something else to say about me: 'He enjoys a challenge, and I don't see him coming back to us until he has succeeded [in rugby union]. He still has a few hurdles to jump.'

Shane put his finger on it there. So to answer the question of whether I enjoy playing rugby union: yes, I do enjoy playing it. I love the way the game flows. I love the science of the game, especially the backline moves. Those moves gave me no end of trouble to begin with, but once I got the hang of them I found that being part of them, fitting into them, was a lot of fun. I love the international side of union and everything that goes with that. And, as Shane Edwards said, I love the challenge of trying to succeed in a different code against the odds.

Only now that my Super 12 debut is on the board can I honestly admit I started out in rugby thinking, "What the hell have I got myself into?" I was a willing party to all the media talk and hype about switching codes, but nothing counts unless you can perform out on the field.

WENDELL SAILOR, WRITING IN THE *COURIER-MAIL*, MARCH 2002.

People have sometimes asked me what I found hardest in union. I can answer that in two parts — off the field and on. Off the field, the hardest thing about switching codes was leaving behind everything that I valued in rugby league. Leaving behind the culture of the Broncos, my profile in the game, the respect I had as a player, the comfort of knowing I was on top of my game. I left all this to go to another game as a 27-year-old rookie, not knowing whether I'd make it as a player, not knowing how I'd be received by the union guys. What I did know was that if I didn't make the Reds' side, which was on the cards, I'd spend the next two years playing club rugby. To go from being the No.1 winger in one code to a club player in another code would have been hard to take.

On the field, what I found hardest was the frustration of not making the impact on the game that I'd been used to making in league. The fact that I touched the ball more often in league had a lot to do with that. In 2002 I went to a lunch held jointly for the Reds, Lions and Broncos. Wayne Bennett was there, and he was asked by the master of ceremonies, David Fordham, what advice he'd give rugby union coaches on getting the most out of me. Benny replied, 'I've said it before: just get the ball to Wendell, just make sure he's got the ball in his hands. That's all you've got to do.'

I know union isn't the same game as league, but I would love to have had the ball in my hands more often in 2002. I don't know how many times I would call for the ball from a breakdown only to have a backrower come around, take the ball and then get tackled. I'd groan with frustration when that happened, because I was used to getting the ball whenever I called for it in the Broncos. In one Reds' match, a backrower came into the backline, took the ball that I had called for and immediately got tackled. Now the fact that I didn't handle the ball more often was partly my fault: I didn't have the instinct to know where and when to go looking for it, as players like Chris Latham and Ben Tune obviously did. I'm confident I'll have developed that instinct by 2003.

I had plenty of problems learning the various techniques of rugby, but, overall, I'd say my biggest problems had to do with learning the backline moves. It was hard enough to remember them, but even harder to run the right lines. One of the Reds would call for, say, a 'coin Bath two' move, and my mind would start racing, trying to remember exactly what move that was. I repeat: the backline moves in union are much more complicated than in league. When I look back on it now, I wonder how I managed to get by in those early Super 12 matches, when I was so raw to the game, such a rookie. Someone asked me not long ago if the Reds designed any special moves for me. I answered no — I just fitted into the moves the Reds already had. The point is that I'm a power winger. Whereas Mat Rogers beats the defence with pure skill. Ben Tune, the other Reds winger, is a cross between the two of us. Tuney has a lot of skill but he's also a bit of a kamikaze when he gets the ball in his hands.

(On the other hand, former Wallaby coach Greg Smith was quoted around the end of the Tri-Nations series in 2002 as saying that Jonah Lomu could no longer rely on his size to get through defenders, because defence in union had improved so much and because the defenders themselves were generally bigger and tougher than they were when Jonah started out. Then Smith said, 'It's the same with Wendell Sailor. He makes some nice breaks, some nice penetration, but this isn't just to do with his size. It's got more to do with his talent, his good footwork.' Coming from someone who knew as much about the game as Greg Smith, I was pleased to read that. I was very sad to hear that Greg died a few weeks after the article appeared.)

The breakdowns, which are a part of the game that doesn't exist at all in league, are sure to be a problem for any league player switching to union. I had to learn what to do in and around the breakdowns and how to get back in position afterwards. I put a lot of time into practising what to do after I was tackled. I'm not the first person to have a problem with this after switching codes. Michael O'Connor did, too. I once read that for a while after he switched from union to league he used to release the ball after being tackled, apparently out of habit. This must have embarrassed him no end at the time.

I remember in my very first match for the Reds, against the Waratahs in 2001, how weird it felt having to place the ball behind me after I was tackled. Now it's become second nature to me. In fact, the Reds' assistant coach, Roger Gould, said to me towards the end of my first Super 12 season that my ball presentation was as good as anyone's.

Having gone through the hoops, I consider myself an expert now on the problems that footballers are liable to come up against when they switch codes. In fact, I could write the textbook on it. The first of the problems begins the day you announce that you're switching codes. From that moment on, people assume that your mind is focused not on the time you have left in your present code but on what you hope to do when you go across to the other code. You're aware of this, and because you're worried about what people are thinking, you try too hard and tense up. The result is that your game suffers. This is what happened to me in my last year with the Broncos. I desperately wanted to play well in my last season, but all along I had the thought at the back of my head, 'People are going to think I don't want to be here unless I really have a go and score plenty of tries.' So I tried too hard and didn't play as well as I should have until towards the end of the season.

I thought of this problem when I saw Lote Tuqiri quoted as saying, after he decided to switch to union, that he couldn't wait to play against me in 2003. I knew when I read this that a lot of Broncos fans would be thinking that Lote didn't have his mind on the job at hand, that all he was thinking about was playing union in 2003, and that, knowing this, Lote would be under the same mental pressure to perform that I had been under.

Maybe he was, too, because he didn't have such a great last season with the Broncos to begin with. I told him so the day before a match about halfway through the season. I asked Lote about his form and he said, 'Watch, Del. I'm going to turn it on tomorrow.' I said, 'I hope so, because you've been terrible the last couple of weeks.' We know each other too well for Lote to take this personally. He said, 'I haven't been playing that bad,' and I said, 'You haven't been playing bad, but you've been doing nothing great, either.' He said to me, 'Del, you just be there — just watch.' I did go to watch that weekend — it was only about the second Broncos match I'd been to all year — and sure enough, Lote turned it on. He scored two tries. Wayne Bennett saw me at the match and came up to me, saying, 'Your mate did well,' meaning Lote. I said, 'He turned it on for me.' Wayne replied, 'Well, Del, you should come every week.'

I'm as honest with other mates in the Broncos as I was with Lote. During the 2002 season I phoned Gorden Tallis and said, 'Mate, how bad are you playing!' Gordy said, 'You don't think I'm embarrassed?' He got back at me after that when I'd been dropped from the Wallabies and was playing for the Gold Coast Breakers before crowds of 1000 or less. Gordy phoned one day and said, 'How's rugby union, Del? Been entertaining any big crowds lately?' I just roll with all the punches like these that I get from my league mates. I had an ambition in union which I don't think they really understood, and that kept me going.

Let me talk specifically about a league player who is switching to union. The first decision he'll have to make is which position he's best suited for. That's not as simple as it sounds. For any given position, the roles in the two codes are so different that you can't count on going automatically from your position in league to the equivalent position in union. Even in my case, there's been talk in some quarters about whether I should be playing on the wing. More than one person has even suggested to me that I ought to have a go at blindside flanker. The idea is that I'd be good at taking the ball up and breaking the line, like David Lyons.

It's an interesting thought, but I think I'll stick to the wing. Apart from anything else, it's the easiest position on the rugby union field for a league player to learn, and I've already spent more than a year learning it. Learning to play as a forward would be another thing altogether. There's so much technique and know-how involved. In union, forwards and backs are different breeds. When I joined the Wallabies I couldn't believe how much full-on physical contact there was between the forwards at training. The forwards used to bag us backs as pretty boys at training because we didn't go in for the same full-on contact. On one side of the field we'd be practising our backline moves, and on the other, people like Owen Finegan and Toutai Kefu and David Lyons would be bashing each other, and others (such as George Smith) would be practising cleaning blokes out. It was all pretty brutal, and I didn't mind at all being on the other side of the field.

Actually, there is another position in union that I'd love to have a go at — fullback. I'd love to have the freedom that full-backs have to insert themselves into the play and run with the ball. That's probably why Jason Robinson, a winger in league, moved to fullback when he played for the Lions against the Wallabies last year. But as much as I'd enjoy playing fullback, I'm afraid my kicking game wouldn't be good enough — I'd be found out pretty quickly.

I've said before how hard it is for a league player to learn to tackle union-style. In fact, I found this as hard to master as anything else I had to do. When you tackle in union, you don't only have to bring the runner to ground; you have to either turn him and hold him up or pilfer the ball, which can mean jumping up as soon as you've done the tackle and trying to get the ball. For some reason, I found this really difficult, and I'm afraid it may have affected my defensive play generally.

On the other hand, the convert to union will find certain things easier. Training is one of these. I referred earlier to the fact that union players spend more time on skills training and less on physical training than league players. In league, you regularly get driven at training to a point where you feel completely stuffed — a dozen 400s followed by eight or nine 100s … that kind of thing. The idea behind it is to make you not just physically fit, but mentally strong, too. I remember doing pre-season training with the Broncos a few years ago at Kelvin Grove in Brisbane at the same time as the Reds. We were training so hard, running a series of 400s, that we could hardly breathe, and we looked across and saw the Reds playing touch football or practising moves and not even puffing. When I joined the Reds in 2002, I found some of the boys remembered the time the two teams trained alongside each other. 'Gee you blokes were training hard that day!' they said.

What of the play during a game? What will the convert from league notice first? If the player switching to union is a back (which he is more than likely to be), the first thing he'll notice when he gets the ball is that he has less room to move. In union, the defence will be on to him quicker and in bigger numbers, which isn't surprising considering that in union you're also up against the two opposition flankers. In league, what I used to love was having the ball kicked to me and then counterattacking with plenty of space to move in. In union, that hardly ever happens. This is another reason why the idea of playing blindside flanker wouldn't appeal to me. I wouldn't like getting the ball around the scrum or ruck, as blindside flankers do, with defenders all around you.

A lot was made of the fact that I didn't once put boot to ball in all my Super 12 matches. The idea put around was that I was a typical leaguie — long on brawn and short on skills, particularly kicking skills. It's obviously true that league players don't kick as much. Some league players are fantastic kickers: Andrew Johns and Darren Lockyer, to name just two. Trent Barrett is a big kicker of the ball, too. One difference between the codes that I noticed is that in union everyone kicks at training because everyone is supposed to be able to kick. In league, you don't kick at training unless you're a designated kicker.

The media talk about me not kicking wasn't a criticism that I worried about. As one of my trainers said to me one day, the fact that I hardly ever kicked was a plus for me, because it showed I was backing myself with the ball in hand. It's not that I can't do it — the fact is I can kick when I need to. It may not be one of the strong points of my game, and I might not be in the same class (as a kicker) as Chris Latham or Matty Rogers, but I can certainly boot a ball 30 or 40 metres down the sideline. If I don't do it, it's because I don't need to. I'm not the only one like this. Ben Tune doesn't kick much, and I've hardly ever seen Jonah Lomu kick. I remember watching Jason Robinson playing for the Lions at fullback in one of the Tests in 2001 and noticing that he kicked the ball only once — and that one kick was a shocker. I've scored tries with chip kicks in rugby league, and I did chip once in the second union Test against France in 2002.

Another thing anyone switching codes needs to be careful about is saying anything critical in public about the code he's just left. It can be taken the wrong way. I learned this at State of Origin time in 2002. I was quoted in a Sydney newspaper saying that the NSW team was the worst I'd ever seen. The result was that the NSW and Queensland players both had their backs up over it. After NSW won the match, Alfie Langer phoned me and said, 'Thanks a lot, Del. Next time do you think you could pump the NSW boys up a bit more?'

A few days after that we trained in Sydney alongside where the NSW league team was training. Andrew Johns saw me and called out, 'Hey, Del, is this the worst team you've ever seen?' The truth is I never said it was the worst NSW side I'd ever seen. What I said was that NSW was an inexperienced team and that if I was still playing for Queensland I'd be quite confident going up against them. The lesson I learned was watch what you say about your former code, because people can resent it if they think you're having a go at them. It doesn't do anybody any good: it just gets you into hot water.

I'd also suggest to anyone switching codes that they follow my example and not try to change their personal style to conform with the code they're going to. I didn't change one bit — I was as cocky and talkative as I'd ever been — and this didn't bother anyone. Once, after joining the Reds, I was talking aloud to myself at training, as I often do, saying, 'Big Del's goin' real good today.' One of the other Reds heard this and came up to me, saying, 'Del, you're a breath of fresh air here.' I had others say the same thing to me during the season. They liked me being myself.

If a player switching to union happens to be a winger, he'll notice one other thing straight off: he'll see a lot less of the ball than he did in league. This was certainly true for me. Earlier in the book I referred to the fact that when I played for the Reds I touched the ball not much more than half as often per match, on average, as I did when playing for the Broncos. This is why some people, including journalists and a few of my former league mates, seemed so keen to see me playing for the Brumbies instead of the Reds — the Brumbies had a reputation for getting the ball out wide.

While on this subject, let me say again that I have the utmost respect for the Brumbies. I admired them years before I thought of switching to union, because I could tell just by watching them on television that they had a team culture like the Broncos. After talking to Peter Ryan, who played for both the Broncos and the Brumbies, I was sure about this. Having now seen them at close quarters and played against them, I know a lot about the Brumbies' team culture. It's the reason they're so close, just like the Broncos. And like the Broncos, the Brumbies totally believe in themselves.

It's true, as I said earlier, that Canberra's cold weather turned me off, but otherwise I think the Brumbies would have been ideal for me — except that I am a Queenslander, 100 per cent. This made all the difference, and I have no doubt I made the right decision by joining the Reds. The funny thing is that guys like Jeremy Paul, Justin Harrison, even George Gregan, still say to me, 'What a pity you didn't play with us for the Brumbies — you would have loved it.' I would have loved it, too — but I loved playing with the Reds more.

WAS IT ALL
WORTHWHILE?

After I was dropped from the Test side Gorden Tallis was quoted as saying that the ARU had bought me as a publicity machine and now that I'd drummed up the publicity that rugby union needed I was being dumped. A Sydney *Sun-Herald* sportswriter, Greg Prichard, asked John O'Neill of the ARU about it. This is what O'Neill said in reply: 'Gorden must have had his tongue in his cheek. Former Broncos players are naturally fantastic with the fans. Wendell adds between 3000 and 5000 to the gate. When the ball goes to him the crowd roars and the people really want him to do well. He's a character, and the story about him swinging the turnstiles at Ballymore and saying "watch these babies swing when Del sells" is terrific. We're looking for a long-term return from him as a player.'

I don't think there's any doubt that I did attract publicity to rugby union. The Reds attracted bigger crowds in 2002, and I was given some of the credit for that. Later, as the Tri-Nations series was getting under way, the *Sunday Telegraph* in Sydney reported the results of a survey of how many times big-name union players had been mentioned in the press since the end of the NRL season in 2001. The firm that did the survey, Media Monitors, found that I'd had 530 mentions, which was 39 per cent of the total and a lot more than anyone else. The next most mentioned player was Mat Rogers, who had 326 mentions, 24 per cent of the total. After him came George Gregan with 170 (13 per cent), Matt Burke 122 (9 per cent) and Toutai Kefu 116 (9 per cent). The *Sunday Telegraph* story said I'd been 'the most talked about player in rugby every month since last October'. It said that in my peak month, June 2002, which was when I made my Test debut, I'd had 128 mentions in the press. June 2002 was also Georgie Gregan's peak month for mentions in the newspapers. His total for the month was 29.

Now I'm not trying to suggest because of all this that I was a bigger star in union than George Gregan or Matt Burke or Toutai Kefu. That would be crazy. These three players were bigger stars in rugby union than I could ever hope to be. I'm just saying that there was obviously heaps of interest in the fact that a high-profile league player like me had switched codes, and I'd like to think I earned my keep as a union player by attracting the interest. But did I really say, 'Watch these babies swing when Del sells'? Well, I did say something like that.

This is what happened. I was talking to a few other Reds at pre-season training one day about the ticket prices that year, and I remember telling them to watch the turnstiles swing when 'Del sells'. It was really just a joke about how the media seemed to expect me to pull big crowds. The quote 'watch these babies swing when Del sells' later appeared in a newspaper and was picked up by other parts of the media. Maybe I did say 'babies'. It sounds like me.

Well, the turnstiles did swing, and maybe the ARU did get its money's worth from me. In fact, a media analyst named Deborah

Lanyon, who was quoted in the *Sunday Telegraph* story I referred to before, made exactly this point, saying that the ARU had already got back the investment that it made in Mat Rogers and me. She said, 'The ARU would see the offering of large contracts as small change for the subsequent media coverage and interest generated for the sport as a whole.'

The Queensland Rugby Union hoped for a crowd of 13,000, with about 3000 of these spectators coming to say, "Hello Sailor" to rugby's latest recruit. The crowd was 14,136. The 4000 or so spectators Wendell Sailor pulled through the gates at Ballymore represented about $100,000, a significant chunk of what Sailor will cost the QRU each year. Money well spent.

SPIRO ZAVOS, WRITING IN THE *SYDNEY MORNING HERALD* AFTER SAILOR'S DEBUT MATCH FOR THE REDS, OCTOBER 2001.

I hope that what Deborah Lanyon said is true. For me, though, the down side was the extra pressure the media attention put me under. Eddie Jones and I spoke about this more than once. It's well known in both codes that if you do more than a certain amount of marketing and promotion it will have a negative effect on the way you play. Wayne Bennett was aware of this, too, because it was a problem the Broncos sometimes came up against. There is no doubt I was under more pressure in 2002 than I've ever been under in my life, but I can't say for sure what effect this actually had on my game. I do know it inhibited me and made me overcautious — to avoid making mistakes — and it probably affected my game in other ways as well.

People have the idea that I'm a showman, and it's true in a way, but the publicity work I really like doing is not corporate work but working with kids — visiting them in schools and hospitals. I get a kick out of seeing the way kids react to me. But at the end of the day, I'd much rather be scoring tries and playing for the Wallabies than attracting crowds and generating publicity. I doubt whether the media will be so interested in me in 2003 — after all, they'll have Lote Tuqiri to talk about — and I'm looking forward to playing without the pressure of 2002.

All in all, I hope the ARU is happy it signed me on. The other side of the question is: at the end of the day am I happy that I threw in my lot with rugby union? Was it all worthwhile? At a personal level the answer is definitely yes. I got far more satisfaction from becoming a dual international in 2002 than I would have if I'd stayed in league and had another big season with the Broncos and Queensland's State of Origin team. I was proud that I'd taken the gamble of moving to union and that the gamble had paid off. Some of the other Wallabies seemed to appreciate this, too. Several of them — Justin Harrison and Jeremy Paul are two I remember — went out of their way to say how much they respected me for leaving league while I was at the top of my game and taking the risk of trying to make it in union, a game I knew next to nothing about. Coming from the people it came from, this was the best sort of compliment I could have received.

Looking back, I think what kept me going after I decided to

switch codes was having to prove to myself that I could do it. I'll admit that there were times when I wondered if I'd made the right decision, like when I said goodbye to the Broncos. I had a lot to be grateful to them for, because the club had given me the opportunity to become who I was. After we lost in the preliminary final against Parramatta, I went around the dressing room and thanked the guys, one by one, for all they'd done and for being such good mates, and I became so emotional as I was doing it that I started to cry. We were now out of the competition, and I suppose I realised at that moment that I would never put on a Broncos' jersey again. Gorden Tallis got a bit upset, too. I'm just so pleased that the football I played for the Broncos in the finals in 2001 was about the best of my whole career.

So leaving league wasn't easy. There were plenty of heartaches and doubts. But more than a year later, I know I did the right thing. I know it has been worthwhile. In spite of what Gorden Tallis said about me returning to league, there is no way I'll ever do that, as much as I'd love to play league again. You have to understand where Gorden is coming from. He admires many of the union players, but he's a league man through and through, and I know he's sour at rugby union administrators for poaching league players, especially fellow Broncos like me and Lote Tuqiri. So if Gorden can say something that upsets the union people in some way, he's happy to say it.

But I didn't appreciate him beating up that story about me, saying that rugby union was about to dump me and that I might be returning to league. The story was thrown up at me at, of all places, a Wallaby dinner at Coffs Harbour. A rugby commentator said to me, 'There's a story going around that you're not happy in rugby union and that you're going to make the move back to league! He also said that the Broncos' chief executive had said they'd welcome me back. I was staggered, and asked where the story had come from. He told me he thought it came from the Broncos themselves. After a few more inquiries, I discovered that Gorden Tallis was behind it.

I was dirty at Gorden for causing me the embarrassment, and I phoned him. I said, 'Mate, what are you doing to me?' He told me not to take it seriously, that he was just joking. I said, 'Well, mate, don't.' I also told him he ought to try to get over the problem he has with rugby union. The union boys are aware of it. 'What's wrong with Gorden Tallis?, they asked me. 'Why is he always having a shot at rugby union?' My reply was that Gorden was very loyal to anything he belonged to, in this case rugby league, and that he didn't mind stirring up a bit of controversy. I also said that Gorden was honest in his beliefs, a straight shooter. He is, too.

Being dropped from the Wallabies before the Tri-Nations series was a big disappointment, even if I was really just giving the right wing position back to Ben Tune when he returned to the team. Nobody ever likes being dropped, and it wasn't something I was used to, because I hadn't been dropped from an Australian team since 1994. What I personally found hard to deal with was training my backside off with the Wallabies until three or four days before the Test, only to be told that the team was un-changed and I'd have to go back to playing club rugby. I'm not complaining about it, because it's obviously something that has to happen, but it's a big let-down for the player concerned when it does.

If someone were to ask me what I liked most about rugby union, I'd probably say it was the game's international dimension, particularly the concept of Super 12. I loved playing against the best athletes in South Africa and New Zealand. I also love the concept of the Tri-Nations tournament, and I can't wait to play in a Tri-Nations Test myself.

As far as on-field play is concerned, what I like most about rugby union is that the game can flow, that it doesn't stop after every tackle as it does in league. I love it when the phases keep rolling, as they did in the second Test against France. It's a pity this doesn't happen more often, because it's what the spectators like to see and what the players enjoy doing.

When I look back on my first full season of rugby, I'm amazed at the number of people in the game who put themselves out to help me. I'm thinking of the blokes I played with, who made me feel welcome, who were always ready to show me what to do and who put up with all the mistakes I made, both at training and in matches. I'm thinking of Eddie Jones as Wallaby coach. I've written a lot about Eddie elsewhere in this book, so all I'll say about him here is that he was very patient with me, as a novice to the game, and was always encouraging and supportive.

I'm also thinking of my Reds coach in 2002, Mark McBain. I owe him special gratitude, because he was the one who gave me my first opportunity. Mark took a chance on me right at the start, when plenty of other coaches would have had me sitting on the sideline until they were certain I was ready. Mark didn't owe me any favours and he definitely wasn't under pressure to pick me first-up for the Reds — I know that for a fact — but he still took the gamble. After I was selected in the Test side, I phoned to thank him, because I owed my place in the team to the trust he'd shown in me. Mark is a great bloke, and I wish him well.

SWITCHING CODES: WHAT LIES AHEAD?

As far as I know, I'm the first league player in Australia without any background in union to switch to union at the elite level, which makes me a kind of pioneer. I may be the first, but I definitely won't be the last. I'm not saying that league players will ever go across to union in droves. That will probably never happen, so I don't think league has anything much to worry about. But I do think a pathway to union has now been opened up that other league players can use, knowing that the switch to union can be made successfully.

How many league players will follow me to union? I often get asked this, and I always say that it's a question I can't answer. I don't know, and I don't think anybody else knows either. Obviously, there'll always be a limit to the number of league players that union wants to recruit. After all, at this moment Australia has only three Super 12 teams. Also, some of the players that union might want to recruit wouldn't want to leave league anyway. Even if the ARU offered him a $5 million contract, I don't think Gorden Tallis would ever switch codes.

However, I have been wrong before when I've made this type

of prediction. I didn't think Lote Tuqiri would switch, for instance — at least not in the next four or five years. He did say to me one day, 'Watch out, Del: I may be over there in the next year or two', but I didn't take him seriously. I knew Bob Dwyer had spoken to Lote about joining the Waratahs as far back as 2001, but I honestly believed he would stay with league for years to come. I've been fairly close to Lote and I was pretty sure I knew what his intentions were. We roomed together in my last three years in league, both with the Broncos and with the State of Origin team, and we became good friends off the field. Tara became very friendly with Lote's girlfriend, Rebecca, too. Anyway, he's a great player, and I think rugby union is very lucky to get his services while he is still so young.

Whether a player makes the big decision to switch from league to union or union to league depends on the individual — what he wants to get out of life, what his plans are, where he sees himself ending up in football. It's really a lifestyle choice, and this is what makes it so hard to predict how many players are going to switch codes over, say, the next 10 years. In the end, a decision whether or not to switch codes is a purely personal issue; it's not a financial one.

In the old days union players had to go to league if they wanted to earn money from their sport. They didn't have any choice. Now, money isn't much of a factor. I can't imagine any player going from one code to another now just for the money, because the money on offer in one code is probably not much different from the money on offer in the other. I can't believe anyone would uproot themselves and take the gamble of succeeding in the other code just for, say, an extra $50,000 a year. People have suggested I switched to union because I was offered a big contract. What nonsense! In spite of what the newspapers said, the difference between what I could have earned by staying with the Broncos and what I earned by switching to union wasn't all that much. As if I'd have given up everything I had at the Broncos and put my future and my family's future on the line for a small pay rise, most of which would have disappeared in tax, anyway. If all I'd wanted was a pay rise, the sensible thing would have been to stay in league and play in England.

As I say, it all comes back to the individual and his personal agenda. Money will mean more to some people than others. When Nathan Blacklock switched to union in 2002, he obviously didn't do it for the money. On the contrary: he was losing a lot of money by switching. He gave up a half-million-dollar deal over two years in league to sign for $130,000 or less in union. It's the same with Matty Rogers: he was offered more money by the Bulldogs than by the ARU. (He's said to me since how lucky he is that he didn't take it.)

Darren Lockyer was offered a lot of money to play league in England and I believe he was also approached by the ARU about switching to union, but he knocked the offers back and kept playing with the Broncos. He said no. I said yes. This has nothing to do with whether one code is better than the other. It has to do with what each of us wants to achieve, what our personal ambitions are, where we want to end up when our playing days are over.

Will most of the recruits from league continue to be players with a background in union — players like Mat Rogers or Duncan McRae or Lote Tuqiri? I'd like to know the answer to that myself. Obviously, blokes with a background in union will find it a lot easier to make the transition. Even if they haven't played union for years, they're sure to pick it up again. For blokes like me, whose background is just about 100 per cent league, it's hard work filling your head with things you have to know about union and then trying to remember them as you play. And if it was hard for me, a winger, imagine how hard it would be for a forward. Imagine how hard Gorden Tallis would find it if he had to play blind-side flanker in a Super 12 team, talented player though he is.

On the other hand, I've demonstrated now that it can be done — that a player raised entirely on league can make it in union. So maybe this will encourage others like me to do the same thing. I'll be interested to see.

There are some league players who I think could make great union players if they have the patience to master the finer points of union. In union, everything depends on timing. In league, the players just want to get the ball and go at it as hard as they can for 80 minutes. Gorden Tallis, who has all the credentials to become a champion in union, is one who may not have the patience for learning the intricacies of union. He certainly doesn't have the patience to watch blokes kick. He once said to me, having a shot at union, that he thought we shouldn't worry about scrums and line-outs and backline moves. He asked, 'Why don't they just give the ball to Elton Flatley and Andrew Mehrtens, or whichever players are kicking, and let the rest of the blokes stand around all day and watch them shoot for goal?'

Not so many years ago, certainly for a few years after I joined the Broncos, 'switch' would have seemed a dirty word to league players if it meant switching to union. After union went professional and began to expand its following, the idea of switching became more acceptable. But there are still league people who resent the fact that union has been poaching some of its best players. I think this is an attitude that will eventually fade away as league people come to realise that poaching one or two players a year doesn't do league any serious harm. League has so much young talent that every time a star player leaves to go to union there will be an 18-year-old or 19-year-old with just as much talent ready to step up and fill his place.

Where league could have a problem is if its rising stars, as opposed to its established stars, start going across in numbers; that would really undermine the game. I'm sure this is why there was so much concern in league circles when Lote Tuqiri decided to go, because Lote was only 22 and still on his way up. So far, Lote has been the only player of that type that league has lost, and he may be the last for some years. League people will be hoping so.

I still have league people say to me that I have turned my back on the game. Naturally, I don't see it that way. Rugby league was very good to me, but I think that after nine years with the Broncos I can say that I served my time and put a lot back into the game. I see myself as a sportsman who is just continuing to play sport, not some kind of traitor.

My old Bronco team-mate Brad Thorn was one forward who did try to make it in union. So far it hasn't worked out for him, and I think that's because he hasn't been patient enough. He didn't have the patience to make all the adjustments you have to make when you switch codes, especially if you're a forward. Everyone knew he had the ability. He was big, quick and talented, a great athlete. His team-mates in the Crusaders had no doubt about that, and they obviously wished he hadn't dropped out of the game in 2001. After our match against the Crusaders, Andrew Mehrtens came up and asked me if I'd heard from him. He was sorry Thorny wasn't around. I was told that Thorny was a great man to have in the club as well as being an awesome player on the field.

I also spoke after the game to Crusaders' winger Caleb Ralph. He said that if Brad Thorn had had a little more patience he would have become a top All Blacks' backrower and might have been one of the stars of the 2003 World Cup. I hope Brad comes back. Switching to union was a big gamble for him, and I really admired him for being brave enough to do it. He didn't only put his reputation on the line: he also took a huge financial risk, because I'm sure he was on big money in league. I know there was at least one other rugby league club that would have paid anything to recruit him, but Brad had his mind set on going to union.

One matter that I think deserves to be sorted out, assuming that in the years ahead a few other league players switch to union, is whether they should be picked for representative teams after they've made their decision but before they've left league. I feel the league needs to decide on a policy here. It was a problem I ran into. A number of league commentators — I think Ray Hadlee was one of them — argued that I should be left out of both the State of Origin team and the Australian league team in 2001 because I'd aligned myself with union. If they were saying this because they looked on me as a traitor, then I think they were small-minded. If they were saying it because they honestly believed that league needed to look to the future and choose a player who would be around for a few years, then I accept that they had an argument. I could understand where they were coming from, but my view was that if I was good enough I ought to be picked. Fortunately, I did get picked.

Can the two codes ever get together and cooperate in some way? My own opinion is no. I believe the cultures of rugby league and rugby union are just too different, and the two codes too set in their ways for either to give enough ground for some type of compromise. In any case, I can't see rugby union ever wanting to do a deal with league. Maybe something of that kind will happen in England. League clubs there have been buying union clubs, and there's talk of the two codes coming together in some way. I can't see it happening in Australia, though. The codes here are too far apart. They're too dyed-in-the-wool.

THE BEST
IS YET TO COME

I believe my first year in rugby union has set me up perfectly for the big year ahead, 2003. It's the World Cup year, and I'll be pulling out all stops to play for the Wallabies. Before that, I'm looking forward to what I hope will be a big Super 12 season with the Reds. The fact that the Reds' new coach, Andrew Slack, said publicly that he had a lot of confidence in me gave me a lift. When he was asked by the media if I was likely to get the ball more in 2003, Slack said he thought that to some extent this was up to me. I had to feel comfortable enough in the game to insert myself into the play, he said. Speaking of me, he said, 'This year [2002] he tended to hold back, wondering should I or shouldn't I, whereas I'll be encouraging him to have a go. That may result in him making the odd blue or two, but he won't be shot for that, I can guarantee you.' I was very pleased to read that — in 2003 I won't need much encouragement to have a go.

I'm champing at the bit to get back into the Wallaby team, because I know the best is yet to come. I haven't the slightest doubt that by the time the internationals begin in 2003 I'll be a much, much better rugby union player than the Wendell Sailor who played those two Tests against France in 2002. One reason I'm confident is that I really feel I know the game well enough now to play it automatically. I won't have to be thinking every moment of the game about whether I'm in the right place at the right time and doing the right thing. In particular, I now feel I know the backline moves. I'm confident now of being where I'm supposed to be. I also know which moves are going to work for me and which aren't, which I think is really important.

The other reason I'm confident is that I'll be back to the physical condition I was in when I played for the Broncos. My weight should be down to 106 kilograms, and I'll be as fast as I ever was. I believe I was in my best-ever physical condition at the league World Cup in 2000. In late 2002, spurred on by Eddie Jones, I threw myself into heavy training after the season ended. I not only began training again with the Broncos, but I stepped up all my own training, and I even doubled my boxing sessions — from one a week to two. By late in the year I was just about back, physically, to where I was two years earlier, at my peak.

Because I believe I played to only 60 per cent of my ability in 2002, this leaves a lot of room for improvement. Nobody can play to 100 per cent of his ability, but I believe I can play to 85 per cent of mine, which means I'm looking to lift my game by more than a third before the World Cup. I'll be so much more confident than I was in 2002. I know the game, I know what's expected of me, and physically I'll be in my best shape. I'm ready for 2003.

I'm certain the Wallabies can win the World Cup again in 2003, even though there's probably more to beat than there was in 1999. England will be strong, and so will South Africa, but I still think the All Blacks will be the team to beat. I've come into contact with their coach, John Mitchell, and I thought he was pretty switched-on. But my money's still on the Wallabies. I feel about the Wallabies the way Wayne Bennett made us feel about the Broncos. If we are to win, we'll have to play to the best of our ability, but if we do play to the best of our ability, nobody can beat us.

Highly paid convert Wendell Sailor is excess baggage on the Wallaby tour as the world champions ignore the power running of the former Kangaroos' Test star. Sailor knocked out Ireland's Dennis Hickie with his first genuine touch of the ball in the Dublin disaster on Sunday – a 23rd-minute crunching as an attempted tackle on the ex-Bronco was met with a hip to the head. But as the Australians battle midfield-meltdown, with the ball failing to reach Sailor on more than a handful of occasions in two Tests, British critics claim the Wallabies are wasting their investment in the Queenslander. Former Welsh great Jonathan Davies has led the chorus, suggesting Sailor is fast becoming the Invisible Man on a $700,000-a-season salary. 'Wendell Sailor may as well not have been there for all the use they made of him,' Davies wrote.

PETER JENKINS, WRITING IN THE *DAILY TELEGRAPH* AFTER AUSTRALIA'S LOSS TO IRELAND IN DUBLIN, NOVEMBER 2002.

I expect big things of the Reds in 2003, too — both for myself and for the team as a whole. The Reds have always had a team of great players, but they've struggled to make the Super 12 finals because they tend to drop games that they really ought to win. Then, when the pressure's on, they're just as likely to win six or seven in a row, as if to show how good they really are. I put all this down to mental attitude. If the Reds had to play the Waratahs every week of the Super 12 competition, they'd win the competition, because they'd never lose a match. This is because they believe in themselves when playing the Waratahs, but against other teams, Otago or whatever, they're not so confident. I've been around top-level football long enough to know about this. I can sense this lack of confidence long before we run on the field. What we need is a team culture like the Broncos — a culture that gives us complete faith in ourselves, which makes us really believe that we can beat anybody when we play well.

I have a feeling that all this will come right in 2003 and that the Reds will go really well. I hope to play a part in that success. One thing I can guarantee: I won't be waiting again until the seventh match of the Super 12 competition to score my first try. I may even do some kicking. After the 2002 Super 12 season, the assistant coach, Roger Gould, who had a great boot himself, said to me that in 2003 we'd work on some chip-and-chase plays off my left boot. I look forward to that.

On the domestic front, too, 2003 promises to be a special year for me. Tara is due to have our second child in mid-January. We're both delighted.

Funnily enough, ever since I arrived on the rugby union scene in Australia, people have wondered how soon I'd be packing up to go somewhere else. I'm not just referring to all that media speculation which Gordy Tallis whipped up about my returning to the Broncos. There's also been talk that I intend going overseas to play rugby — to France, Japan or somewhere — as soon as the World Cup in 2003 is over.

This is rubbish. Imagine me giving up all that I'd achieved in rugby league for two short years on the international rugby scene, the first of which was really just a learning year! Let me state here that I'm in rugby union for the long haul. It gave me a bit of a shock the other day when I realised that my career as a professional footballer is already 10 years old. Ten years! It's gone so quickly. I want to make the most of the years I have left. I intend to see out my football days in rugby union, eventually hanging up my boots around the age of 34 or 35. By then, I'll have had nine years in league and seven or eight in union.

Switching to rugby union has opened up a new world for me. I wasn't feeling stale playing league, but somehow the challenge of making it in the other code has given me a huge lift. It's freshened me right up. As I prepare for 2003, I feel more positive and more focused than I have ever been in my life. I'm proud that I've already become a dual international, but I don't want to go out as a Wallaby who played only a couple of Tests. I'm like a kid who's been given a few lollies and wants more. When I sat on the sideline at the Tri-Nations Tests, I felt exactly the way I did when I sat on the bench at the 1993 league grand final. I promised myself then that I wouldn't be sitting on the bench next time, and I made myself the same promise in 2002.

Like league, rugby has offered me the chance to play before big crowds, earn good money and represent my country. There may be a better way than this to make a living, but if there is I have yet to hear of it. There's nothing I like better than running out to play in front of a big crowd. The bigger the better, as far as I'm concerned. There will be very, very big crowds in 2003.

I'm looking at a four-year career as a rugby international, which means I have three to go. I want to be in the Wallaby mix. I want to become a permanent fixture in the Wallaby line-up. When the Wallaby team is announced, I want Wendell Sailor's name to be there.

Let's see what happens.

INDEX

Akermanis, Jason 152
AMI 42, 44, 49, 109
Anasta, Braith 179
Anderson, Chris 34, 35, 37, 38, 51, 52
Arthurson, Ken 14

Barrett, Trent 33, 94, 177, 195
Beetson, Artie 69
Bennett, Wayne 17, 18, 19, 20, 21, 23, 25, 26, 30, 38, 39, 40, 41, 43, 44–49, 52, 65,
    79, 89, 90, 91, 93, 94, 95, 123, 143, 157, 158, 169, 170, 173, 174, 179, 180, 181,
    182, 183, 185, 189, 192, 200
Blacklock, Nathan 14, 207
Bond, Graeme 105, 122
Boston, Billy 39
Bowman, Tom 96
Burgess, Mark 139
Burke, Matt 123, 134, 184, 199

Campese, David 103, 108–113, 117, 129, 130, 132, 143, 178
Carne, Willie 15, 26, 62
Carozza, Paul 22
Carroll, Tony 22
Chappell, Greg 143
Civoniceva, Petero 177
Cockbain, Matt 85
Cockerill, Richard 28
Collins, Barry 27, 42
Connell, Cyril 62, 170
Connolly, John 112, 123, 140, 143, 144
Connors, Mark 17

Cordingley, Sam 84, 85, 142
Cribb, Ron 98
Croft, David 76, 154
Croker, Jason 93

Daley, Laurie 89, 93, 94
David Campese Management 42, 108–109
Davies, Jonathan 214
Dwyer, Bob 117, 119, 131, 206
Dyson, Fletcher 76

Eales, John 11, 26, 27
Edwards, Shane 187, 188
Ella, Glenn 145
Ettingshausen, Andrew 47

Felingham, Chris 65, 66
Finegan, Owen 24, 91, 150, 177, 181, 193
Fittler, Brad 90, 154
FitzSimons, Peter 129, 131
Flatley, Elton 106, 137, 145, 208
Fordham, David 189
Freeman, Cathy 46, 68

Gee, Andrew 23
Gidley, Matt 36, 37
Giles, Kelvin 62
Gillmeister, Trevor 153
Gould, Roger 84, 96, 191, 215
Graham, Richard 96
Gregan, George 24, 70, 71, 87, 91–93, 109, 123, 124, 126, 164, 165, 180, 181, 197, 199
Grothe, Eric 36, 37
Growden, Greg 74, 76, 117, 118, 138
Guinness, Rupert 79, 80

Hadlee, Ray 210
Hancock, Michael 48
Harrison, Justin 168, 197, 201
Hawse, Adam 79
Herbert, Anthony 83, 84, 125
Herbert, Daniel 16, 78, 85, 97, 123, 124, 157, 163
Hickie, Dennis 214
Horan, Tim 154, 157, 172
Hughes, Merv 75

Jenkins, Peter 214
Johns, Andrew 15, 33, 86, 123, 154, 176, 177, 179, 195, 196
Johnson, Martin 28
Jones, Eddie 17, 19, 24, 44, 45, 46, 48, 50, 111, 121, 122, 127, 128, 129, 130, 131, 132, 133, 135, 137, 138, 144, 154, 164, 168, 173, 174, 178, 181–186, 200, 204, 213
Kearney, Stephen 36
Keenan, Greg 109
Kefu, Steve 105
Kefu, Toutai 17, 104, 126, 157–159, 175, 181, 193, 199
Kershaw, Gerry 36
Kimmorley, Brett 36

Langer, Allan 20, 21, 22, 23, 24, 30, 65, 69, 95, 123, 149, 196
Lanyon, Deborah 199, 200
Larkham, Stephen 87, 109, 123, 127, 137, 168, 176
Latham, Chris 17, 78, 85, 104, 107, 112, 113, 114, 154, 155, 156, 160, 161, 180, 189, 195
Lazarus, Glenn 42
Lee, Phil 149
Lee, Renee 149
Leeds, off-season at 27–29
Lewis, Johnny 66
Lewis, Wally 16, 78, 105
Lloyd, Leon 96
Lockyer, Darren 17, 21, 24, 33, 38, 94, 123, 124, 129, 176, 177, 182, 195, 207
Lomu, Jonah 97, 125, 131, 133, 140, 143, 144, 162, 163, 190, 195
Love, Martin 58
Lyons, David 122, 193

McBain, Mark 73, 74, 77, 79, 82, 83, 84, 100, 102, 104, 116, 119, 181, 204
McGiffin, Peter 57
McGraw, Daryl 108–110
Macqueen, Rod 24, 44, 45, 131
McRae, Duncan 26, 207
Maher, Jimmy 58
Mascord, Steve 36
Mayerhofler, Mark 125
Media Monitors 199
Mehrtens, Andrew 176, 208, 209
Messenger, Dally 13
Miller, Jeff 48, 49, 119, 134, 147
Mitchell, John 213
Morgan, Garrick 93
Mortlock, Stirling 133, 134, 155
Mundine, Anthony 15, 66, 68, 159

Nalatu, Ricky 82, 84
Nicholas, Ryan 124

O'Connor, Michael 111, 172, 173, 191
O'Neill, John 147, 198

Paul, Jeremy 197, 201
Pelesasa, Junior 84, 118
Picone, Anthony 44
Prichard, Greg 198

Ralph, Caleb 210
Ramsamy, Jason 134
Rauluni, Jacob 84, 85, 102
Renouf, Steve 70, 142
Ribot, John 38
Ricketts, Steve 39
Roberts, Ian 66
Robinson, Jason 133, 137, 144, 161, 162, 193, 195
Robinson, Keith 98–100
Robson, Frank 57, 62
Roe, John 17, 117, 118
Rogers, Mat 14, 16, 80, 111, 115, 117, 122, 123, 126, 127, 132, 134, 153, 159–161, 177, 178, 190, 195, 199, 200, 207
Ryan, Peter 23, 45, 91, 174, 197

Sailor, Alison (mother) 35, 43, 51, 54, 55, 58, 63, 64, 71, 129
Sailor, Daniel (father) 12, 43, 51, 53–59, 63, 64, 68, 69, 102, 129, 130
Sailor, Michelle (sister) 56, 64
Sailor, Tara (wife) 32, 41, 46, 51, 65, 75, 77, 101, 115, 129, 146–151, 215
Sailor, Tristan (son) 65, 68, 71, 146, 148, 149, 151
St Patrick's College, Mackay 62, 168, 170
Seymour, Brett 168, 170
Shaw, Tony 22,
Slack, Andrew 22, 120, 212
Smith, Darren 91, 100
Smith, George 193
Smith, Greg 190
Spencer, Carlos 124
Staniforth, Scott 105, 115, 119
Stcherbina, Marc 105, 115
Stiles, Nick 175, 180
Stransky, Joel 28
Symonds, Andrew 58

Tallis, Gorden 17, 21, 22, 24, 31, 33, 34, 38, 39, 40, 41, 47, 62, 66, 94, 101, 129, 157, 158, 167, 170, 175, 182, 185, 187, 198, 202, 203, 205, 208, 216
Tallis, Wally 170, 176, 192
Thompson, Adrian 84
Thorn, Brad 209, 210
Treacy, Darren 100
Tucker, Jim 80–81, 89, 96
Tune, Ben 11, 15, 18, 78, 82, 86, 104, 121, 122, 132, 133, 134, 144, 155, 162, 168, 182, 183, 184, 189, 190, 195, 203
Tuqiri, Lote 14, 21, 94, 112, 123, 129, 142, 162, 177, 178, 191, 192, 201, 202, 206, 207, 209

Umaga, Tana 109

Van Vollenhoven, Tom 39
Vernon, Dennis 101, 147

Walker, Andrew 15, 26, 83, 92, 111, 127
Walker, Chris 142, 162, 185
Walters, Kevin 30, 42, 54
Webcke, Shane 21, 24, 38, 39, 175, 182
Weidler, Danny 122
Whitaker, Chris 111, 117, 118, 119
Wilkinson, Jonny 137
Wilson, Jeff 92

Zavos, Spiro 125, 126, 200